9/92

WALTER HAMMOND

By the same author:

Learie Constantine (The Cricket Society Literary Award, 1975)
Village Cricket
Cricketer Militant: the life of Jack Parsons

From Chatham to Churchill
The Story of Health (with Anne Howat)
Dictionary of World History (ed.)
Documents in European History, 1789–1970
Oxford and Cambridge Schools Examination Board, 1873–1973
Stuart and Cromwellian Foreign Policy
Who Did What (ed.)
Culham College History

WALTER HAMMOND

GERALD HOWAT

London
GEORGE ALLEN & UNWIN
Boston   Sydney

**George Allen & Unwin (Publishers) Ltd,
40 Museum Street, London WC1A 1LU, UK**

George Allen & Unwin (Publishers) Ltd,
Park Lane, Hemel Hempstead, Herts HP2 4TE, UK

Allen & Unwin Inc.,
9 Winchester Terrace, Winchester, Mass 01890, USA

George Allen & Unwin Australia Pty Ltd,
8 Napier Street, North Sydney, NSW 2060, Australia

First published in 1984

British Library Cataloguing in Publication Data

Howat, Gerald
  Walter Hammond.
1. Hammond, Walter   2. Cricket players –
Great Britain – Biography
I. Title
796.35'8'0924   GV915.H/
ISBN 0–04–796082–5

Set in 11 on 13 point Garamond by Nene Phototypesetters, Northampton
and printed in Great Britain
by Butler & Tanner Ltd, Frome and London

For Valerie, his daughter

Contents

Illustrations

Acknowledgements

The biographer cannot walk alone. In his journey he seeks the company of those who knew his subject. To make their acquaintance renders his task a pleasure and gives profit to his book.

My quest took me to meet those who played cricket with Walter Hammond or watched him; who were his friends in childhood and adult life; who were his colleagues in the Royal Air Force and in business. For the value of their conversation, let me thank the following: G. O. Allen, CBE; L. E. G. Ames, CBE; T. E. Bailey; X. Balaskas; C. J. Barnett; His Grace the Duke of Beaufort, KG, PC, GCVO; Haydn Bradfield; J. H. Britton; Patrick Compton; A. H. Coy; J. G. W. Davies, CBE, DLitt.; W. J. Edrich, DFC; J. H. Fingleton; Charles Fortune; Miss Kathleen Goodworth; N. G. Gordon; Hugh Gormley, formerly Chairman of Dunlop (South Africa) Ltd; Mrs Joyce Gracie; T. W. Graveney, OBE; R. E. Grieveson; J. Hardstaff; The Hon. Dr Owen Horwood, Minister of Finance, Republic of South Africa; Sir Leonard Hutton, Kt; J. T. Ikin; Sidney Levey; Professor Gavin Maasdorp of the University of Natal; Michael May; Alan Melville; F. W. Mills; Bruce Mitchell; W. T. Moore; Alan McGilvray; G. W. Parker; G. H. Pope; H. E. Pope; Mrs Grace Quick; T. L. Robinson, TD; Mrs Anna Ryly; R. G. Sinfield; E. W. Swanton, OBE; Mrs Muriel Taylor; E. Tranter; P. Van der Merwe; Bruce Vester; W. Voce; Boon Wallace; C. Washbrook; Peter Webb; Miss Ursula Wicks; Mrs Joan Wilkins; G. H. Wills; Mrs Noël Witchell; John Woodcock; R. E. S. Wyatt; N. W. D. Yardley; D. M. Young.

Among over 200 correspondents, I am especially grateful to the following: Gillie Andrew; Wing Commander D. Annand; The Rev. P. D. S. Blake; Sir Donald Bradman, Kt; J. F. Burrell; Group Captain Jack Butterworth, CBE; Professor James Davidson; A. K. Drew; Flt Lt W. G. Fell; Brigadier R. C. Halse; H. J. Hill, MBE; Harold Larwood; T. B. Mitchell; Squadron Leader A. S. Mould; W. J. O'Reilly; J. F. Reece; Air Marshal Sir Anthony Selway, KCB, DFC; J. B. Stollmeyer; B. H. Valentine; A. E. Wilson.

Various institutions made their resources available to me and my thanks are due to Gloucestershire County Cricket Club and especially Graham Wiltshire, Deborah Morgan and Bert Avery; to the BBC and especially its officials at the Written Archives Centre in Reading and the Sound Archives Centre in London; to the Marylebone Cricket Club and especially Stephen Green, the librarian; to staff at the Bodleian Library, Oxford, the British Museum Newspaper Section at Colindale, London, the Bristol City Library and the Ministry of Defence.

I regarded a visit to South Africa as essential since Hammond spent the last years of his life there in a country he had visited as a player on several occasions and where he served during the second world war. Those whom he knew and whom I met are acknowledged above. There were others who in various ways also helped to make my visit beneficial and enjoyable. I was shown round all the former Test grounds, given access to records and offered hospitality. I would like to thank Douglas and June Bossenger (the parents of my son-in-law), their daughter Jill (who arranged my itinerary), Erica Mitchell (who invited so many Springboks to meet me), Helen Horwood, Jane Maasdorp, Margaret van der Merwe and Vivienne Elkington.

I am also grateful to the Department of History in the University of Natal who invited me to lecture while I was in Durban and to the South African Broadcasting Corporation who invited me to broadcast in Johannesburg and in Cape Town.

South Africa was where I met Mrs Sybil Hammond, her son Roger and her younger daughter, Valerie. Their recollections of husband and father were generously offered. To meet the three of them was the centrepiece of my research and I am immensely grateful for their co-operation. I am delighted that Valerie allowed me to dedicate the book to her.

There are others whose help came to me in a variety of ways. In the collection and preparation of photographs I was aided by Norman Lilley, of the Queensway Studio, Thame, David Frith, editor of *Wisden Cricket Monthly*, Richard Wilson of Kodak Ltd, and Nigel Taylor who negotiated on my behalf with the *Sydney Morning Herald*. To their contributions may be added those of Major E. J. Chapple, who tracked down surviving pupils from Cirencester Grammar School, Christopher Ducker of the *Bristol Evening Post*, Robert Hallam, treasurer of the Walter Hammond Memorial Trust Fund, and Kelvin White who interviewed Jack Fingleton for me in Canberra. Derek Lodge and Philip Bailey, of the Association of Cricket Statisticians, checked the details of Hammond's career.

My manuscript was read by Max Reese, G. O. Allen, Grahame Parker and Sir Leonard Hutton. I am grateful to them all and especially to Sir Leonard for kindly writing a Foreword.

There are three final debts: to John Newth, senior editor of Allen & Unwin, whom I first met on the cricket field twenty years ago and who has seen the book through the press; to Anne, my wife, who accepts me retiring to my study to write books and whose sound judgement converts the 'purple passages' to balanced prose; to Carole Gilbert, who has acted as my secretary over many years. She has handled all the correspondence, collating, indexing and typing involved. Without her efficiency, reliability and serenity it would not be possible for me to combine authorship with another professional career. As the director's name comes last, and most important, in a list of film credits, so let hers be the last in the list of my acknowledgements in this book.

North Moreton   GERALD HOWAT
Oxfordshire
1983

Foreword

by Sir Leonard Hutton

Gerald Howat has written an outstanding and delightful book about one of the greatest cricketers the game has ever seen, if not the greatest. He brings the reader very close to a rather difficult subject, for Walter Hammond was a man who kept his thoughts to himself or to his few close friends. This book brings to light his early life, his days as a young professional and his successes. The author tackles carefully the problem of how he coped with success.

I consider myself very fortunate to have played with and against Walter Hammond. In the 1930s he was in a class of his own whether batting, bowling or fielding. He made a very difficult game look like child's play and it was no wonder that he created an enormous amount of jealousy amongst those who were not quite so well endowed. As a very junior member of the Yorkshire team I would hear comments from some fine cricketers, who sang Wally's praises when they said he was a great player. I knew he was something out of the ordinary, for Yorkshiremen do not praise easily.

I looked forward to my first meeting with the great Gloucestershire and England cricketer with eager anticipation. The match was at Gloucester and I had my first view of the world's finest cricketer as a bowler. I was able to watch his beautiful action as he bowled to my partners. From the start of his run to the delivery of the ball he looked the complete athlete. Had he so wished, I am sure Hammond could have been an outstanding bowler. His action was one which all young bowlers could emulate. I remember seeing him bowl leg-breaks and googlies on one occasion during the MCC South African tour of 1938–39.

It was, however, as a batsman that the genius of Walter Hammond stands out like a star on a black night. He was the finest batsman that I played with or against. Two century innings against Yorkshire, one at Bradford, the other at Bristol on a wicket taking spin, were masterpieces. I was at Lord's in 1938 to see his double-century against Australia. This elegant, powerful innings stands out for me today just as clearly as when it was played over 40 years ago.

I was fortunate, very fortunate, to share several long partnerships with Hammond. I was able to study his technique at close quarters in the middle and I was also able to study this great cricketer in the dressing room. I liked him very much. I liked his modesty. I never heard him say an unkind word about anyone. I learned a lot from him simply by watching him, not by what he said, for he was like Wilfred Rhodes in this respect. Neither said a great deal about cricket; both were very modest and helpful in their way.

It was with a certain amount of trepidation and apprehension that I looked forward to partnering Hammond at the wicket in a Test match. What if I ran the great man out? That would be dreadful. My imagination pictured confusion and fear, but my fears were unfounded. The several partnerships which I had with Walter are some of the happiest memories of my cricketing life. He was a good runner between the wickets, with no dashing here or dashing there, no shouting: it was a run or not a run. Of all the batsmen I shared the crease with, he was the easiest of partners.

Walter Hammond on all wickets was the finest batsman against whom I played. He could hit the ball as though it had been fired from a gun. He could make spin-bowlers on a turning wicket look inept. He made 50,000 runs in first-class cricket, usually without bothering to play the hook stroke. I am sorry that the young cricketers of today are unable to see two hours of Hammond at the wicket. I thank him for the pleasure he gave to me and, I am sure, to many thousands of cricket lovers the world over.

I enjoyed reading this book immensely. It is a very good book indeed, and it brought back for me many happy days in the sun. I was lucky to have played with Hammond and to have made two overseas tours with him as captain. I also remember meeting his son, Roger, when he came to spend a day with my family. I enjoyed the son's company as much as I enjoyed his father's. They were both charming people. I am very glad this book has been written about a cricketer who, on all types of wickets, had no superior.

Kingston-on-Thames   LEONARD HUTTON
1983

1

Soldier's Son, 1903–20

'The boys were enthusiastic at the prospect
of seeing their champion Hammond giving
their paters an afternoon's leather-hunting'.
Wiltshire and Gloucestershire Standard, 1919

The Gloucestershire XI were licking their wounds on Friday 19 June 1903. It was raining and the county side spent the day in the Tonbridge pavilion reflecting on their dismissal by Kent the evening before for 31 runs. Gilbert Jessop had been their top scorer with eight. They missed W. G. Grace, who had left them to captain London County.

A few miles away from Tonbridge the rain fell also in Dover, obscuring the high chalk cliffs and the castle on the hill with its massive keep. Within the castle grounds a young corporal went anxiously about his business. He spent the morning instructing in musketry but his thoughts were elsewhere. In the married quarters his wife was giving birth to a son. To the illustrious names of Jessop and Grace, Gloucestershire would one day proudly add that of Walter Hammond. Kent, their opponents on that June day in 1903, would not secure his services despite his Kentish birth. Indeed, the name 'Hammond' had more Kentish associations than with any other county. Fourteenth-century Kent provides records of seven times as many men with a similar name as in any other English county. Its origins lay in the Old German word Haimo, meaning 'a home'.

Corporal William Walter Hammond was born in Hampstead on 14 January 1879. His father, Robert, was a builder. Hampstead doubled its population in the last quarter of the nineteenth century, and there was plenty of work to be found in building houses to fill the open spaces of West Hampstead. William grew up there, benefited from the compulsory elementary education required by the Mundella Act of 1880, worked for a few years in an office, then enlisted as a clerk in the Royal Garrison of Artillery on 14 December 1897, just a month short of his nineteenth birthday. Three years later he was promoted corporal.

The reforms of the 1870s had made an Army career a reasonable prospect for young men such as him with an artisan background. Learning from the lessons of the Crimean War and watching the successes of Bismarck's Prussian troops, British politicians had modernised equipment and given some self-respect and dignity to the ordinary soldier. He was no longer, as the Duke of Wellington had once said, 'the scum of the earth'.

The newly developed modern Army was first put to the test in the Boer War in South Africa, but Corporal Hammond was not called upon to serve in the country where his son would eventually spend so many years of his life. Instead had come a posting to Dover Castle as an instructor.

With a regular saving of two or three pounds a month and with the chance of a married quarter, he was in a position to get married. He had met in the village of Buckland, a few miles from Dover, Charlotte Marion Crisp. The Crisps lived at 18 Grace Terrace and Marion's father was a railway clerk. They were both 23 and were married in Buckland Parish Church in December 1902. They set up home in a quarter on the first floor of the flint-stone buildings overlooking the keep. Their quarter was approached up a metal staircase and through a heavy wooden door. Inside were four rooms, two on each side of a corridor – gaunt, austere and even primitive – yet the one in which Walter Hammond was born had already made history. Set incongruously against the drab surroundings was a plaque on the outside wall commemorating the fact that George III had once rested in that very room. George's father, Frederick, had some claims to being an eighteenth-century royal patron of the game of cricket. The son of the twentieth-century corporal of artillery would make a magisterial contribution.

The child was christened Walter Reginald in the Garrison Church of St Mary-within-the-Castle in a robe lent by the Dentons. Corporal Arthur Denton and his wife Florence were close friends of the Hammonds. Their son, Dick, was just a few weeks older than Walter. Florence's sister, Dorothy, was married weeks older than Walter. Florence's sister, Dorothy, was married to William Moore, the Regimental Quarter Master Sergeant. The three families, all posted to the castle together, saw a lot of each other in the confined conditions of Service life. The Moores were an old Army family; William Moore's father, as a Master Gunner, had taken part in the siege of Sebastopol and had survived the Charge of the Light Brigade.

Corporal Hammond and Corporal Denton were both keen on sport and their two sons, Walter and Dick, were playing cricket in the keep-yard as soon as they could hold a bat. The space was 30 feet across and the gun-wharf door provided a formidable wicket.

All too soon, the two families and the two little boys went their separate ways. Dick showed himself to be an able pupil, passing on to Dover Grammar School and winning a scholarship to Selwyn College, Cambridge. His career lay in the colonial service and the two boys seldom met later. But Dick had been no mean first sparring partner for the future England cricketer. His cricket won him a place in his college side at Cambridge and a surviving picture shows him hurdling against the distinguished Olympic athlete, Lord Burghley.

Walter had been a precocious little cricketer at Dover, for at five he left with his parents for Hong Kong. Yet those early games at the castle, with Dick bowling and a little girl called Ellen Taylor remembering (80 years later) that she was allowed to field, need not be discounted completely. He once said to a mother whose five-year-old boy came to him for coaching, 'We've missed the three important years!'

Of the family's short spell in Hong Kong on the China Station no record survives beyond that of William Hammond's promotion to sergeant. But a clearer picture of Walter's childhood re-appears when the family went to Malta in 1911, staying there until 1914.

In Malta, a white bungalow with a typical Maltese-style flat roof became their home at Sliema Barracks. The barracks themselves were large, impressive and elegant. Malta had been a British possession since 1814 after a long and chequered history of many masters. The barracks epitomised the importance of Malta within the British Empire. Soon the island would acquire a new role as squadrons of the allies anchored in its harbours during the war which broke out in 1914.

But thoughts of war were not in the minds of the ordinary

serving soldier in the last days of the Edwardian era. Life at Malta offered lots of sport, regattas and entertaining. Wives and children were part of this active scene. Even the annual camp, when troops moved out of barracks and went under canvas on the neighbouring island of Gozo, was a holiday outing for families. Fathers were responsible for keeping an eye on their own households in a separate set of tents. One task was to clear thistles which shot up overnight before tender feet crept out from under the canvas.

Christmas brought a different scene when servicemen's children went to a party at Government House given by the Governor, the Duke of Connaught. There were some 60 children from the Sliema Barracks and one of them, Anna Gaulding, whose father was a fellow-sergeant with William Hammond, remembered these occasions as she did the little school which they all attended. It was in a wooden hut which became the church on Sundays until a garrison chapel was built. The teachers were all Army instructors. She clearly recalled Walter as a 'demanding small boy' who was forever pestering everyone else to play cricket. At break-time he would rush out with a bit of chalk, mark a wicket, grab a bat and summon someone to bowl. The bowlers might be boys or girls: it was immaterial. Anna Gaulding bowled him many a ball without getting much of a bat in return. He was a boy who 'could get other children to do anything for him. There was no question of his being a bully.' Yet he was undoubtedly displaying the first signs of those qualities of dominance in the things which mattered to him.

There were very few weeks in the year when cricket could not be played but when summer was at its hottest even he was ready to take part in the boating trips to Valetta which were organised for the children and in the swimming parties off the beaches. One less official enterprise was picking figs in a churchyard near the barracks. It was fun while it lasted but the children were stopped because the place was full of the graves of cholera victims.

One great occasion was the visit of the hero of the Boer War and the founder of the Scout Movement, Sir Robert Baden-Powell, in 1912. The 1st Sliema Scout Troop were on parade. Nine-year-old Walter stood, staff in hand, haversack on back, as the great man inspected the troop of which the boy's father was scoutmaster. Brigadier Richard Halse remembered the enthusiasm with which Sergeant Hammond ran his troop and had 'vivid recollections of myself, as an eight-year-old, and Walter learning semaphore on the barrack square.'

All this was left behind when the Hammonds sailed for England just after war broke out in August 1914. Running the gauntlet of German U-boats, 46th Company of the Royal Garrison Artillery sailed through the Mediterranean, the Bay of Biscay and the English Channel to become, in France, the 116th (Heavy) Battery. Marion Hammond bade her husband farewell, settled herself in Southsea and sent her son to school at Portsmouth Grammar School.

Of Walter's days there, Edward Wilson, a contemporary in the third form in 1916, wrote some recollections which remain in the school archives:

He was about 13 years of age, with dark, curly hair, a sun-tanned, freckled face, and unusually powerful chest and shoulders, due to much diving and swimming in Malta. It is no exaggeration to say that for sheer physical strength he was half as strong again as a normal boy of his age and size. Many opponents fielding at mid-off or cover point have wrung their fingers as a searing drive from his bat came their way. During his last cricket season at school, he played regularly for the 2nd XI. He was also a wonderful dribbler on the football field whilst in the fives court he would astonish us with spectacular overhead hitting.

He disliked school work as heartily as he loved games, and it was this that started our friendship. I happened to be near the top of the class, and he pleaded with me to help him with his homework. The difficulty, of course, was to give him enough assistance to escape detention, but not enough to arouse his masters' suspicions. After steady tuition along these lines, he progressed sufficiently to average about 13 marks out of 20. In return, he undertook to persuade the team selectors to put me in the 3rd XI – his idea, not mine, as I was well below 3rd XI standard.

He also gave me some cricket coaching on Southsea Common during the long evenings of the summer term. His idea of fielding practice was to stand 30 yards apart and hurl the ball at one another's ankles. At first I thought this unnecessarily brutal, but I soon found it less trouble to stop the ball than to keep running after it. Undoubtedly, this stern training helped me when I reached the 1st XI.

Wilson took a snapshot of his friend, surely the only picture to be found of him with dirty pads, no batting gloves, tousled hair and ill-fitting shirt! But look at the left elbow, the right shoulder and the eyes in photo no. 4.

Marion Hammond had rented rooms at Capworth House, King

Street, Southsea. Her husband was in France throughout the war, becoming Battery Sergeant Major and being commissioned in the Royal Garrison Artillery in 1915. He was involved in the greatest battles of the war and by July 1917 had been promoted major. The decision early in 1918 to take Walter away from Portsmouth Grammar School and send him to Cirencester Grammar School in Gloucestershire was therefore one primarily taken by the boy's mother, who felt he needed the stability which the boarding facilities offered and the companionship which it was difficult for him to have at home. She had also begun to consider what career the boy might one day pursue. Cirencester had close links with the agricultural community and, more particularly, with the agricultural college just outside the town. Farming for a lad of strength but without intellectual attainments might be the answer. Walter took with him to his interview at Cirencester testimony to his abilities as an athlete, and the headmaster, Timothy Frazer, willingly accepted him into the boarding house.

Cirencester Grammar School had been re-built in 1880 at a time when many a town and country grammar school, with origins going back two or three hundred years, was being revived after the Report of the Taunton Commissioners on Secondary Education. Such schools offered, for modest fees, a sound preparation for university, the professions, business or farming to the children of the locality they served. At the time Walter entered the school there were 300 pupils, boys and girls, of whom 50 boys were boarders. Schools such as this were small enough to create a real identity of interest for their pupils, to inspire loyalty and to foster active old pupil associations.

So, on 18 April 1918, Walter changed schools and faced the adjustment to a new environment, fresh friends, different teachers and strange pastures. Within days of beginning to make this adjustment, he was brought to the headmaster's study to be told of his father's death. On 5 May 1918 Major Hammond was killed in action in the heavy fighting near Amiens.

Excitement at allied successes on the Western Front and the evident prospect of Germany's defeat had little appeal for the fourteen-year-old boy. The war might end tomorrow but it had cost him his father and left his mother widowed. After a few days at home, he returned to school and began to make his mark in various sporting activities. He came fifth in the school endurance swim, completing 870 yards. He also won the diving prize for his age-group.

In his first winter term in the school he helped the boarders to win the House Trophy at football for the first time for many years and secured a place in the school 1st XI. The 'characters' feature in the *Cirencestrian* reported:

> Outside right, but can play in any position. Is speedy, and exercises wonderful control over the ball. Can kick from any position, and is a fine shot. Probably the best all-round player in the Eleven.

In the summer of 1919 he won a place in the cricket 1st XI. Cirencester Grammar School played other local grammar schools, neighbouring villages and occasional XIs. Scores were seldom high, although in Mr Frazer the boys had a headmaster who was both an enthusiast and a coach. Under his influence Walter was taught, as he himself recalled, 'to go for the off-shots and attack the bowling.'

In the opening games, he usually managed to get himself a mention in the 'line-scores' without achieving anything spectacular. Against the Church Lads' Brigade he made 15 in a total of 81. Against Poulton and Amney St Peter village side he took 6 for 28 and made 29.

But by half-term he had progressed and his all-round abilities were displayed in a game against Marling School at Stroud. He took 5 of the Marling wickets for 52 and then scored 70 of Cirencester's 104. A first-innings lead of 17 runs became a match-winning investment when Marling collapsed for 35. Walter collected four more wickets. Left with a mere 19 to get, the visitors opened with Walter Hammond and Billy Neale. With a greed for the strike which never left him, Walter got 17 of the runs. Marling might, with foresight, have wondered what they had done to deserve two future Gloucestershire players in the opposition. Certainly, they had been effectively beaten by the efforts of one of them. The sun had shone all that June day and at the end of it, as the charabanc made its way back to Cirencester in the late evening warmth, Walter must have felt that he had skills of considerable quality. Billy Neale, as W. L. Neale, would become a stalwart of the county side between the wars.

In July 1919 came the Peace Celebrations. The school participated in the combination of parades and church services which up

and down the country marked Britain's celebration of the confirmed end of hostilities. During the week the school arranged
a match with the Parents. The *Wiltshire and Gloucestershire
Standard* reported that 'the boys were enthusiastic at the prospect
of seeing their champion Hammond giving their paters an afternoon's leather-hunting.' Alas, he was bowled off his pads second
ball and the boys were all out for 53. But he and Neale ensured that
this was enough, the two participating in the fall of all 12 Parents'
wickets for 46 in this 13-a-side game. So finished the season in
which he had scored nearly 600 runs and taken 86 wickets. His
batting average of 45 was scarcely approached by Neale (12) and
by no-one else at all. He ended the term by winning some events in
the swimming sports and passing into the fifth form to be a candi-
date for the School Certificate.

Another successful football season followed and in 1920 he
captained the cricket XI in a season in which his personal
dominance was established from the start. No opponents were
safe from the onslaught of his batting or the effectiveness of his
bowling. On one occasion the school XI, chasing 89, were all out
for 40, Walter batting through the innings for 36 not out. The
village of North Cerney were devastated by his 6 for 22 following
his innings of 70 in a school total of 122. The pattern repeated itself
throughout the summer: 67 out of 86, 45 out of 73, 38 out of 59,
61 out of 76, and 101 out of 153.

Training for Sports Day provided some alternative to cricket.
Walter, on the day itself, won the Mile in 5 minutes 55 seconds, the
100 yards in 11·4 seconds, and the Long Jump. He threw a cricket
ball 96 yards to win that event also, as he did the 440 yards, the 220
yards handicap, the cross-country and the hurdles. His long jump
was a new school record, as was his throwing of a cricket ball.
It goes without saying that he was declared Victor Ludorum, far
outstripping in points his nearest opponents.

Then came an innings of 44 in a school match which had some
bearing on his future. The opposition were styled The Comrades
of the Great War XI and captained by a county player. Walter, not
out on 44 at tea, heard him remark, 'That boy may go to Australia
one day.' Pride or lack of concentration had their reward when he
fell to the first ball after tea but the conversation encouraged the
headmaster to write to Gloucestershire about his young protégé.

The 1920 school season ended for him in a blaze of glory. He
made no mistake in the Parents' match. At tea he was 62 not out

with the hope expressed in the speeches at this social occasion that he would go on eating. He chose to go on batting instead and made his first century. The Parents, with their strongest side for many years and including several local club players of repute, were dismissed for 52, Walter taking 6 for 16.

This was followed by a house match in which he had the 'gigantic' score (as the local *Standard* phrased it) of 365 not out. The innings, comprising 24 sixes and 38 fours, was made in one hour and 54 minutes. In a small school, where at the level of 1st XI he was a colossus, there was obviously little to fear in the mixed bag of performers who would bowl in house matches. Then, as now, the raising of house teams can lead pressed men onto the cricket field to make up the numbers. But even in the most advantageous circumstances, 365 runs still have to be hewn out of the rock of opposition bowling – and bad balls can get wickets. It was an innings which nearly did not happen. On the morning of the match he was given detention but a tolerant geography master agreed to let it take effect a day later. But for making such a large score he was excused the detention altogether.

His school career was over. The *Cirencestrian* published averages in which the first and second places tell their own tale:

FIRST ELEVEN

Name	Runs	Batting Innings	Not out	Top score	Average
W. R. Hammond	752	18	5	110*	57.84
A. Leadbetter	110	15	1	48	7.86

	Overs	Bowling Maidens	Runs	Wickets	Average
W. R. Hammond	163.4	41	327	81	4.04
B. Wilkinson	19.4	1	49	10	4.90

HOUSE MATCHES

	Innings	Batting Runs	Not out	Top score	Average
W. R. Hammond	4	613	3	365*	613.0
W. E. Smith	4	51	1	27	17.0

	Overs	Bowling Maidens	Runs	Wickets	Average
W. R. Hammond	32.5	11	50	25	2.00
W. E. Smith	41	9	68	18	3.77

The 'characters' feature acknowledged that he was 'without doubt the best cricketer ever produced by the school' and commended his captaincy. The headmaster declared at prize-giving that the school had been fortunate in having such 'an exceedingly good athlete who during the past season had achieved a certain amount of notoriety.' Fame would have been a happier choice of wording, for clearly he wished to say nothing but good in the young man's favour, adding that he had 'no doubt he would be greatly successful' in the forthcoming Cambridge Locals Examination Results.

Yet it must be said that Walter had not been tested in the context of really good schools cricket. Cirencester's opponents were not schools of any great cricketing stature. On the doorstep were Cheltenham, Clifton and Marlborough but none of these public schools would include a small country grammar school on its fixture list. Cirencester Grammar School played its fellow grammar schools, technical schools and the local villages. The future would show if Walter's exceptional talent at the level he had played would be sustained.

How had this outstanding athlete fitted into the life of the school? How had his contemporaries remembered him?

His performances attracted the inevitable hero-worship. A schoolfellow wrote to the national press with full details of the 365 to match the achievement of some other boy's 372. Walter himself displayed an indifference to such admiration which was taken by some to be conceit or arrogance. Only the more discerning spotted the shyness which, throughout his life, made him shun publicity. Girls rather than boys, even in a school where the sexes were kept apart in a way unthinkable 60 years later, got to know him. School dances were popular occasions and Hammond, known as a good dancer, was much in demand.

The teaching staff handled this remote, rather lonely, pupil well. The headmaster, ready to give praise when it was due on the appropriate occasion, treated him with firmness in other areas of school life. He was aware that Walter was no scholar but was determined to get some work out of him.

Boarding houses in schools in the 1920s lacked frills. Indeed, part of their objective was to offer a Spartan training. Walter was grateful for occasional outings to the Neales' farm at Berkeley where he was sometimes invited to stay for a few days in the holidays. Billy Neale remained one of his lifelong friends.

Another future friend met him soon after his father's death in May 1918. Freddie Mills, an old boy, turned up one day at school on leave from the war. Mills called on the headmaster to pay his respects, enquired about the fortunes of the cricket XI, and was invited to 'look over a promising youngster who'd just joined the school.' He saw Walter batting in the nets, had a word or two with him, and made a mental note to watch him over the next two years. The war, Mills guessed, had not long to run and soon he would be back putting together Cirencester Town cricket. Promising school-boys would be needed.

The meeting came fortuitously for this one particular school-boy, new, strange and stunned by the death of his father. When next he and Mills met, a friendship sprang up which was to last for 40 years. Mills, by 1919 the ex-serviceman back home and starting to earn his living as a civilian, felt that Walter did not seem to have a proper base for the school holidays, beyond occasional visits to the Neale family farm. The boy was glad to accept the hospitality of the Mills' family home in Cirencester, and Freddie Mills' mother and father were delighted to have him to stay.

Why Walter did not go home regularly for the school holidays to his mother in Southsea must remain a matter for speculation. He was all she had and filial duty pointed such a course. Obviously a farm in the country had more appeal than a town flat, but the suspicion lingers that Marion Hammond was already dominating and smothering the boy. At the age of 17 the best way to cope was to keep away, at least for part of the time.

When he was at home he would sometimes go to the house of Harry and Lilian Pannell, friends of his mother. Their daughter, Muriel, was a few years younger than he but a friendship sprang up. To say that she was the sister Wally never had would be to over-state the case, but the two enjoyed each other's company and his earliest games of golf were played with her. The Pannells, like the Neales and the Mills, gave him the family welcome for which he craved. He visited them over the years when playing cricket in Hampshire. Harry Pannell occasionally gave him a pound or two and found £50 to kit him out for the 1925 West Indies trip. The family went to his wedding in 1929 and Harry Pannell, despite being a generation older than Walter, was his best man.

Harry Pannell's advice had been sought when Marion Hammond agreed with the headmaster that Walter should leave. An entry in the school register indicates that he was destined for

Winchester Agricultural College, and his continued friendship with the Neale family had kept alive the possibilities of farming as a career. But within a few days of his leaving school, a different decision was taken.

On 29 July 1920 he left Cirencester Grammar School and two days later made his third separate century in ten days when he appeared for Cirencester v. Stroud. Important as this was in that it represented his debut in men's cricket, it was less significant than his appearance in a Gloucestershire trial a few days afterwards. Mr Frazer's letter and the testimony of others had been heeded. Walter played for a Gloucestershire Club & Ground side against the Old Cliftonians. His 60 runs and two wickets got him an enthusiastic press notice in the *Bristol Times and Mirror* and led to a visit from two members of the committee to his mother in Southsea to discuss her reaction to a professional contract.

He has left on record his impressions of that visit. Etched on his mind was the picture of that agonised hour while his mother weighed the pros and cons of the prospect. Eventually she agreed and the schoolboy of a fortnight earlier signed the contract which at the start of 1921 would make him a Gloucestershire professional.

To sign for Gloucestershire was a passport neither to stardom nor to wealth. The county no longer enjoyed the fashionable reputation it had done in the days of the Graces, it still lived in their shadow, and in 1920 was overdrawn at the bank. The county had 'a past that in the nature of things can never be approached,' recorded *Wisden* a year or so later. 'Whatever the present race of players may do they cannot hope to equal the ancient glories. There will never come another W. G. Grace.' Perhaps not a Grace – no-one else has combined in one person a contribution to the game at once statistical, social and evolutionary – but in the young man who made his county debut at the end of the 1920 season Gloucestershire had found an artist and technician in all departments whose performances on the cricket field in the inter-war years did something to dispel the dismay and uncertainty of the 'twenties and 'thirties. Walter Hammond, we shall come to realise, was not essentially a happy man but he brought a full measure of happiness into the lives of thousands who saw him or followed his fortunes.

2
Young Professional, 1920–26

'A natural cricketer with a great
future before him'.
The *Bristol Times and Mirror,* 1920

Walter Hammond made his debut as a first-class cricketer in Gloucestershire's match against Lancashire at Cheltenham in August 1920, less than a month after leaving school. The start was inauspicious in that it rained all the first day and he was lbw for 0 on the second. Against Leicestershire he made 2, to the chagrin of a charabanc load from his old school. At Worcester he got 18, caught by the old Worcestershire captain, H. K. Foster, playing his last game for the county. But his potential talent had been spotted. The *Bristol Times and Mirror* declared that 'he showed uncommon grit and was not afraid to hit the ball.' He was 'a natural cricketer with a great future before him'. This was high praise and an astute appraisal of his qualities on the strength of 27 runs in four innings.

With the arrival of autumn, Marion Hammond had other plans for her son. He was put to work with Frank Young, a farmer with a smallholding in the village of Alvestone in the Isle of Wight. A few scattered memories of those days have come to light. Farmer Young would go around delivering his produce in the neighbourhood and one villager remembered him speaking of a lad he had on the farm who bowled cabbages like cricket balls. Charles Dore's father ran a small timber business and Walter would wander up to watch the wood being sawn up.

During that winter he played some football for Ryde Sports

Football Club. Whatever further plans there may have been to follow the farming experience with attendance at Winchester Agriculture College never came to anything. When the summer of 1921 arrived, Hammond was back in Bristol ready for the season.

He was found digs in Dowry Road. In the evening he would get a tram home from the county ground and alight near where John Garrod and Bert Pearce had their 'pitch'. After a few nights passing them by with a nod, he stopped. 'You should paint your wickets against that lamp post,' he said 'and measure out a length.' Suiting words to action, he showed the boys what he meant, picked up the piece of wood which served for a bat and joined the lads in their game; even in these lighter moments, it is interesting to see that Hammond made sure he batted first!

The decision taken in 1920 by Hammond or rather his mother, for he was only 17 in a day when parental influence was still considerable, was one of courage and optimism. In joining Gloucestershire he was not linking himself with one of the major counties with a large professional playing strength. Gloucestershire was a side mostly composed of amateurs. In 1921 – Hammond's first full season as a member of the staff – 32 players turned out for Gloucestershire of whom over 20 were amateurs. Only one of the amateurs had any pretensions to being a bowler, and the attack was in the hands of four or five professionals.

The sheet-anchor of Gloucestershire's batting was the professional A. E. Dipper, solid, dependable, accumulative, from whom Hammond learnt much. Charlie Parker and George Dennett were the principal bowlers. Parker had begun his career for the county in 1903. As a left-arm bowler he was probably second only to the great Rhodes in contemporary English cricket. The diminutive Harry Smith was the wicket-keeper. These four men, with a couple in support, represented the professional strength of Gloucestershire.

Hammond, then, as a young professional, would be asked to earn his keep in this company. He was expected to be among the leading run-makers and the wicket-takers. No amateur would appear often enough to establish himself in a particular role in the side. In this Gloucestershire was no different from all but Yorkshire, Lancashire, Nottinghamshire and Surrey. Those counties, with the industrial and commercial wealth of Leeds, Manchester, Nottingham and London behind them, employed large professional staffs. The rest might expect to call upon over 30 men in a summer and retain a minimum of professionals. English county cricket in sides such as Gloucestershire offered a pleasant opening for the talented amateurs who could find leisure from business or professions. It was to remain so throughout the inter-war years and the major period of Hammond's career.

That Hammond's decision called for courage and optimism may also be seen from the state of English cricket as a whole. In the winter of 1920–21 England lost all five Tests to the Australians and in the following summer they lost a further three. The game in England was, for the moment, in a trough of despondence. 'English cricket,' as one judge put it, 'was overwhelmed.'

Hammond saw at close quarters how great those 1921 Australians were. They came to Bristol for their twelfth match, having won eight, including the first Test. On the evening of 7 June 1921 – while still under 18 – Hammond was told he would be making his first professional appearance against them on the following morning. Gloucestershire lost the toss and he watched Warren Bardsley and Charles Macartney contribute centuries to an Australian total of 533 for 8.

Late on the second day he went out with Dipper to face for the first time an Australian attack. The sun shone in a cloudless sky, the ground was packed with spectators. But there was to be no high drama. Moments later, he was trudging back to the pavilion for a single. But the lessons of watching Macartney bat the day before were not in vain. Engrossed in admiration, and learning all the while, he had let a four slip through his feet. He wrote that those conceded four runs were worth many a boundary to him in the years which followed – scored in the manner of the man he had studied.

In August the Australians came back to Bristol. By now the Tests were behind them. Again Hammond was picked, though no county match had come his way in between. School friends from Cirencester came over – members of the XI he could still have been captaining that summer. Again he watched Macartney and Bardsley each make a hundred. He himself fell to a ball from J. M. Gregory so fast that his stumps cartwheeled. To the nought of that innings he added a single in the second. His first-class average at the end of the season of 1921 was 0.66. 'If ever there were a more flattened youth, I have yet to hear of him,' he wrote.

Runs proved easier to get for Gloucester City where he

appeared several times during the summer. The City club, older by some 40 years than the County one, could claim several members who had appeared for Gloucestershire. In 1921 Hammond scored nearly 400 runs for it and made a century against Newport. His bowling was strikingly successful and the club gave him a benefit match which raised £10 from the gate and £6 from a collection. A year later he was again available for the City and averaged over 50 for them. Those games at the Spa, in Gloucester, were a bridge between school cricket and the county game, playing against such sides as Cheltenham, Stroud and Swindon and across and beyond the Bristol Channel to Newport, Hereford and Ross.

His main business that summer of 1921 was to learn his craft and this he did at Clifton College, Bristol, as assistant to the school coach, John Tunnicliffe. Tunnicliffe's cricket went back to the Grace era and he had participated in a first-wicket stand of 554 for Yorkshire against Derbyshire in 1898. He lived to a great age and saw the whole of his protégé's career.

Hammond has acknowledged his debt to Tunnicliffe for his technical advice in the arts of batting and slip-fielding especially. Tunnicliffe constantly emphasised the importance of footwork. 'Get thy feet reet and ball'll do whatever tha wants,' the old Yorkshireman urged. It was Tunnicliffe who also inculcated in his pupil the importance of smartness which he himself had learnt from that martinet of Yorkshire captains, Lord Hawke. When the pair of them were not coaching boys, Tunnicliffe was coaching Hammond. Only when the younger man felt that he was being 'coached out' of some particular shot because it did not entirely match theoretical orthodoxy did he disagree with his master. From Tunnicliffe, Hammond was passed to George Dennett. Dennett was a taskmaster, keeping his pupil at the nets day after day to cure a particular fault but consoling him when he failed against the Australians a second time and assuring him that Gloucestershire meant to keep him. Dennett passed on to Hammond a concern and generosity in the early years that he himself was reluctant (except in writing) to extend to others later on.

During the summer Hammond also paid a visit to his old school to play in the Old Boys' Match. Unfortunately he was caught and bowled by his former cricket master, E. W. Flaxton, for 0. The head-master took the view, so often quoted in relation to W. G. Grace, that the crowd had come to see Hammond bat rather than Flaxton bowl. Nothing could be done but Hammond returned in sub-sequent years to play in the match with more success. In the view of surviving old boys and girls of the school he retained a strong sense of loyalty. He belonged to a generation more ready than later ones to maintain links with school and he was no exception. He took his turn as president of the Old Pupils' Association. 'He felt he owed something to the school,' commented one of his con-temporaries, and he remained its most distinguished old pupil in modern times. The Frazers, the headmaster and his sister, had been kind to him and it did not go unremembered.

After the cricket season of 1921 Hammond signed for Bristol Rovers. Bert Williams, the trainer, was sent to collect him from the station and establish him in new digs in Belton Road. Bristol Rovers had been elected to the newly formed Third Division (South) in 1920. They employed two dozen professionals whom they paid about £5 a week. Hammond, however, only drew appearance money with win-bonuses. His career began in the Reserves in the Southern League, playing on the right wing. During 1921–22 he made four appearances for the first team and in the following season he appeared ten times. His first goal came on 16 September 1922 in a home match at Eastville against Reading before a crowd of 8000 but soon afterwards the *Bristol Times* took him to task for his share in two defeats by Plymouth Argyle within a fortnight. 'The weakness of the side lay in attack and the chief offender was Hammond,' who was duly dispatched back to the Reserves.

Four more first-team appearances came in 1923–24 but no more goals. But modest as Hammond's record was, Bert Williams (whose own career as trainer and official with the Rovers lasted till 1962) believed he had great potential. Williams regarded him as the fastest player he ever knew at Eastville and he and the manager, Andrew Wilson, considered that Hammond had the makings of an international footballer. By 1923 his potential as an international cricketer had been recognised and there were those who felt he might join the very few who had played both sports for England. But Hammond gave up football at the end of the 1923–24 season. The football world was more proletarian than he cared for. He was a little different from the rest of the Bristol Rovers squad. His grammar school background made him socially and educationally superior, his driving of a golf ball out of the football ground won him bets, his speed in circuit-training left everyone lagging behind and his paying the trainer's wife to wash his kit was the grand gesture. After three winters' brief incursion he put the game behind him and concentrated on his cricket. He had taken just £50 from it. Even the digs had not been what he really wanted and he later moved to The Mall in Clifton.

Alfie Stoneham ran a fishmonger's business in The Mall, at no. 32, and he and his wife, Christine, lived above the shop. Hammond stayed with them until he got married. Yet he need not have continued to be in digs at all. Marion Hammond had rented a flat in Bristol to give her son a home, but at the age of 18 he preferred to live with the Stonehams. He cared for his mother and in later years found money to help her. But, as we have already seen, she had the effect of smothering him. He was content to see his mother often enough, though not to be under the same roof. Indeed, her approval was sought for his friendship with the James sisters.

Grace and Gladys James were revue actresses at the Bristol Hippodrome. The Stonehams had taken Hammond to a show or two and the girls, if not the songs, caught his fancy. Soon he met them and, in time-honoured fashion, would wait for Gladys at the stage-door. But Gladys quickly tired of him and passed him over to her sister Grace.

At 22, she was four years older than Walter but found herself attracted to the handsome boy who was painfully shy, tongue-tied and rather gauche. 'There was I, on two pounds a week, kicking my legs in the chorus and with a real boy-friend.'

He remained a boy-friend for six years and a friend for many more. The sisters lived at home with their mother. Walter had been approved of by Mrs Mary James and soon Marion Hammond became a friend of the family as well. The mothers, in those days of the 1920s, acted as chaperones but the travelling lives which both Walter and Grace led gave them plenty of opportunities for independence.

For a spell, Grace was on the London stage. When Walter played cricket or football there, the couple met. Dancing was one of their favourite pastimes at which both were very good. Gate-crashing a private dance was not repeated after they had been told to leave. Grace taught him to sing songs to her piano accompaniment and many a musical evening took place at the Stonehams'. Day-trips to seaside resorts were possible on Sundays in the summer and more often when cricket had ended for the season.

The great Victorian actress, Marie Lloyd, was a friend of Mary

James and would come to stay. Not long before her death in 1922, there sat down to supper the three older women – Marie Lloyd and the two mothers – with the two girls and Walter. The actress did her best to 'bring out' the young man and get him to talk. She won his confidence and gradually he told her of his hopes. 'All that boy of yours wants to do is to hit a cricket ball as hard as he can,' she said to Grace afterwards. The great star of the pre-1914 era, who had commanded £100 a week on the stage in the 1880s, had met, had she but guessed at it, a great star of the future who would fulfil all his ambitions and be as great a household name as she had been. Their meeting must take its place among the list of unlikely such occasions in history.

Shyness and silence in the presence of that supper party can be understood. Yet Walter continued to be shy and silent in Grace's company long after they had first met. The question had to be asked of her, 60 years later, 'Why did you bother with him?'

Grace Quick, in her flat in Weston-super-Mare full of paintings and autographed photographs from the stars of her generation, looked out over the sea-front and thought back over that passage of time.

> He danced well, mother liked him. I liked his mother. He was so handsome, so graceful, so strong. Later on, he got a little car and took me out in it. He was so modest, even when he began to be famous. He liked me because I didn't make him talk about his cricket and because I went to watch. He wanted me in the tea-tent when I was free. If I wasn't there, he often sat in the tea-tent by himself unless his mother came. I was sorry for him. He always seemed so lonely. He wrote such beautiful letters to me when we were apart. I wish I'd kept them all. He was such a clean boy. Never drank; always smartly turned-out. If only he hadn't been so silent, brooded so much, been a bit more humorous. When he nearly died I was at the hospital as often as I could.

The last reference was to his near-fatal illness after the 1925–26 tour of the West Indies. By then, the couple had reached an 'understanding'. The Gloucestershire authorities sent him to South Africa in September 1926 to make a full recovery. From there he cabled home to Grace proposing marriage. Her answer was 'no'. 'In the end, I couldn't bring myself to marry him. He wasn't romantic enough. He had scarcely kissed me in six years.'

A relationship whose foundations were sympathy on one side and dependence on the other might have prospered had not

Grace James's vivacious nature demanded something more. 'Tommy', as she alone had called him, was not broken-hearted, she thought, and he remained a visitor both to the James's home and, in due course, to the married home of Grace and Cyril Quick.

Grace was important. To a young man whose only security lay in performing on a sports field, she was a life-line. Her home gave him the family life for which he so often craved. She met his undemanding emotional needs from soon after the time he left school until just before he met his future wife. Not forgetting his mother and the young Muriel Pannell, we may regard her as the first woman in his life.

Meanwhile, his life as a professional county player had begun in earnest in 1922 when he travelled to Lord's for the second match of the season and scored 32. But the consequences were unfortunate. With the best of intentions, Sir Home Gordon, for many years a critic and observer, mentioned his batting to Lord Harris. That great man, treasurer of MCC and trustee of Kent, had stridden the inner corridors of cricket power for nearly half-a-century and been president of MCC as far back as 1895. Harris discovered that Hammond had been born in Kent and had no title by birth or residence to play for Gloucestershire. To have gone to school at Cirencester was not a residential qualification; nor were holidays in Berkeley. Hammond played a few more games before Gloucestershire were informed that MCC were not prepared to accept his eligibility despite the fact that they had accepted his name at the start of the season as a Gloucestershire player. The press were not aware of the background to this story and, as the *Bristol Times* remarked, 'The identity of the challengers has not been revealed.' But the paper gave a clue why the qualification had been challenged:

> It will be reasonable to assume that Gloucestershire have been penalised because they were the first to recognise that Hammond is likely to develop into a player of outstanding ability, and so prevented him drifting into the service of the county in which he was born, but who have had nothing to do with teaching him the game.

The trail led to Kent and Lord Harris, though some time elapsed before his name was publicly associated with Hammond's disqualification. What remains of interest is that Hammond's talents as 'the most promising professional recruit discovered for many years', as one press report declared, had been spotted on the evidence of a handful of modest innings. The press as a whole was critical of the MCC ruling: 'We want to give all possible encouragement to youngsters who are likely to make their mark in the future and not to put obstacles in their way.'

By now a young critic was making his first cautious forays as a cricket writer, achieving the scoop of a lifetime in 1921 when he, almost alone of the press, witnessed A. C. MacLaren's XI beat those undefeated Australians at Eastbourne. Curiously, the writer had also had a spell as assistant to a famous coach at a public school a few years earlier. Neville Cardus had been assistant to Ted Wainwright, the old Yorkshire cricketer, at Shrewsbury. He too had listened to a purist of the nineteenth century declaring how the game should be played. Tunnicliffe's influence helped Hammond to become a great performer, and Wainwright's helped Cardus to become an astute observer. Some of Cardus's finest prose was reserved for his judgement of Hammond: 'a sculpture of elegance and strength'. Cardus was to believe in Hammond from the moment he first saw him. Hammond's disqualification delayed that moment. Not until 1923 did the Cardus rhetoric meet a subject to whom it could do justice.

Hammond has described his anxiety as the Gloucestershire committee wondered whether to flout MCC and pick him to play against Somerset. Discretion prevailed and he was seen no more for nearly 12 months in the first-class game. And so 1922 became, as had been most of 1921, a season of net-practice and observation. All who came to play at Bristol or Cheltenham were watched for what they might teach the ambitious but frustrated young professional. Probably the best performance he saw was that of Gloucestershire's own Parker taking 9 for 36 against Yorkshire in 70 minutes. A link with Grace was the re-appearance of C. L. Townsend who had played with WG in the county side in the 1890s. A prospect for future English cricket was the sight of Herbert Sutcliffe. The current generation of Test match players was represented by large scores from Patsy Hendren and Frank Woolley. There it all was: a panorama which he might only view, a tableau in which he might not participate, Prometheus chained to his rock.

By the spring of 1923 Hammond had spent 2½ years on the county books for extremely few appearances on the field. Gloucestershire, to their great credit, paid him in full and he was grateful for the fact. The county's first game in 1923 was against Surrey and it proved a magnificent curtain-raiser to the season. Hammond was told to open with Dipper and their partnership put on 180. Dipper fell for 99 and Hammond went on to get 110. A score of 92 in the second innings brought him close to two centuries in the match. 'He had,' said the *Bristol Times*, 'made the future of Gloucestershire far more hopeful.' It was batting with Dipper in that match which taught him the art of running quick singles and impressed on him the need to be physically fit.

The match finished with Surrey's P. G. H. Fender saving the county from defeat and making one of those spectacular centuries that were so much a feature of his career. The game had also given Hammond his first chance of watching Jack Hobbs at close quarters, a player whom he regarded as 'every young batsman's model and ideal'. Not another century came his way that summer.

Early in June came the Lancashire match at Gloucester. A small crowd watched as Dipper and Hammond pursued the 225 runs asked of them. The visitors' attack was in the hands of Cecil Parkin and Richard Tyldesley, two of the best bowlers in England that year, and the chances of Gloucestershire getting the runs on a pitch sensitive to their spin were not great. In the press box was Cardus, now firmly established as the *Manchester Guardian* cricket correspondent and seeing Hammond for the first time. Cardus more than liked what he saw and the public next morning read that there was an England player in the making. Gloucestershire had not won but Hammond had batted with grace and assurance. Henceforth, Hammond was Cardus's man.

Soon afterwards he was seen by another important critic, P. F. Warner, when he played against Sussex. Of a modest 24, Warner wrote in the *Morning Post*:

> I watched Hammond with special interest. He is very young and he has a good style. He stands well at the wicket, with his left shoulder square to the bowler and with his right toe pointing slightly to the left of point, with the result that he gets well over in playing the off-ball and shows the bowler the maker's name on the face of the bat. I liked his cricket immensely.

Other influential people who saw Hammond were becoming convinced of his talent. He was given his first chance in representative cricket when he played for the Players against the Gentlemen at the Oval and scored 46. *The Times* remarked: 'This is a most interesting player. He obeys exactly the canons of nineteenth-century orthodoxy.' Tunnicliffe's coaching was bearing fruit.

He made over 1300 runs that first full summer and *Wisden* wrote of him:

> Here we have in all likelihood one of the best professional batsmen of the future. Irreproachable in style and not yet twenty-one years of age. He has all the world before him and there is no telling how far he may go.

A year later Hammond was feeling depressed at his own performances. The home supporters in 1924 had seen a chain of innings only two of which exceeded 50. 'The more care I took, the worse the results became. Whenever I saw a committee man look at me, I fancied I noticed unpleasant possibilities in his eye.' One county match remained and Hammond was determined to confound his imagined critics. The start was inauspicious. Gloucestershire were all out for 31, the very score they had made against Kent the day before he was born and their equal lowest. Middlesex replied with 74. 'I made up my mind quite cold-bloodedly to get a century,' he wrote, and he did so. His 174 led to a Gloucestershire victory and was, the press agreed, the display of the year. 'He stands foremost among the younger generation of professional batsmen, a performance bordering on the sensational,' said one reporter.

That score of 174 gave him his 1000 runs for the summer. It mattered less than it might have done that he promptly failed against Scotland at Bristol later the same week in a match which the county very nearly lost. Nor, indeed, did he do anything for the Players against the Gentlemen at Blackpool. 1924 had been a wet year, with some counties fearing bankruptcy with so many blank days. Hammond had wanted hard wickets on which to prove himself. Whatever hopes he might have had of being on the boat to Australia were not realised, though Cardus had pressed his claims to be in the England side that summer against the South Africans. Whether he would have helped save MCC in Australia from yet another disastrous defeat can only be conjecture. Brilliantly as Hobbs, Sutcliffe, Woolley and Hendren batted, they could not match their Australian counterparts.

Again in 1925, the Bristol crowds had to wait until August for

Hammond to score a half-century before them. A string of modest scores were only redeemed by 94 and 50 in Cheltenham Week, together with a century against Kent at Maidstone. Hammond, in his own view, 'had not been satisfying' over a long spell. He went to Old Trafford in mid-August for the last county match at that ground, determined to set the record right. Lancashire that year were at the top or thereabouts with three bowlers in Tyldesley, Parkin and Ted McDonald claiming 400 wickets between them.

McDonald, of the 1921 Australians, had come back to England to play League cricket and then join the county. The idea was novel and made no appeal to the purists. Australians were Australians, the argument ran, and there they should stay. The emigration to England of W. L. Murdoch at the turn of the century was different, while W. E. Midwinter had traversed hemispheres so often that it was difficult to remember where he started. Only after the second world war would there be an 'invasion' of the England county scene by overseas players, with implications that could scarcely have been envisaged in the 1920s.

In McDonald, Lancashire had the fastest bowler in England. Bowling slightly short of a length, he presented a severe threat to the average county player, as 182 wickets that summer could testify. But he was made to work for them that day when Dipper and Hammond took the county attack apart between midday and the tea interval. Dipper eventually went for 144, the partnership putting on 330 and breaking the ground record. At the end of the day Hammond was 232 and he batted on until the innings ended the following morning to bring his total to 250. Cardus was there to rhapsodise upon the occasion:

> Yesterday was the gladdest I have spent on a cricket field for many years. The cricketers of Grace's county came to dour Old Trafford and brought with them tidings of joy and comfort. Young Walter Hammond of Gloucestershire played one of the finest innings that can ever have been accomplished by a boy of his age.
>
> To be present at the rise of a star in the sky and to know it is going to be glorious – here is a moment thrilling indeed to men who live their lives imaginatively. It was as plain as the nose on Bardolph's face that Hammond is an England batsman of tomorrow. In years to come we will remember August 19 1925 at Old Trafford for when in good time Hammond carves history out of Australian bowlers here and across the seas, we shall be proud to say that we understood well enough he was born for the company of master batsmen.

Yet even without that 250 he had been noticed that summer by Hobbs who, a few days earlier in the *Weekly Dispatch*, had placed Hammond top in his list of future England players. His cricket was distinguished by 'off-driving and the power and certainty' with which he hit. He was, said Hobbs, 'potentially a very great all-rounder'. Hammond had a chance to watch a lesson from 'the Master' a fortnight later when Hobbs made 266 not out for the Players against the Gentlemen in the Scarborough Festival. Ironically, his own batting was not needed in that match, with a declaration coming in the single Players' innings before he went in.

Hobbs's suggestion of potential rather than performance as an all-rounder calls for comment. In the three full seasons Hammond had appeared for Gloucestershire he had taken just over 100 wickets and in 1925 he had opened the bowling on several occasions. One critic wrote that summer that Gloucestershire were trying to make a bowler of him but he hoped the temptation would be resisted. His concern was not that Hammond lacked the qualities but that he lacked the strength. 'A great batsman and a fielder brilliant in the slips or the covers should not be overtaxed.' This critic and others such as Cardus were nonetheless impressed with Hammond's easy action, rhythm and his ability to swing the ball at a medium to fast pace.

He finished in 1925 by playing in two other representative games. England had a wealth of batting that year, as the averages showed. The top six, Hobbs, Hendren, Percy Holmes, Woolley, Andy Sandham and Sutcliffe, were above 50. Rhodes, not far off his fiftieth birthday, averaged 40. Hammond lay thirty-third in the list with an average of 34. He kept company with men like J. H. Parsons, E. R. T. Holmes, D. R. Jardine and Lord Tennyson. But figures were not the measure of his performance. The English selectors had seen enough of Hammond to include him in the side to tour the West Indies. A party of amateurs, with the leisure to go, needed the assured strength of the professionals accompanying them.

To leave grey English shores in December for the sun-drenched beaches of the Caribbean has become, in the 1980s, within the sights of many a cricket lover. Package tours and air travel provide an opportunity that can be enjoyed by those prepared to save for a winter holiday during a working life or those ready to celebrate retirement. Today's cricketers who go on such tours are used to the energetic support of fellow-countrymen.

It was not always so. The West Indies, even in the 1920s, had not lost the air of magic, the lure of islands with a legend of gold, sugar and pirates which had haunted them since the days of Drake, Hawkins and Raleigh. In the nineteenth century cricket had come to the West Indies through English servicemen and settlers, and just 30 years before MCC's visit of 1925–26 the first English side had gone to the Caribbean.

Hammond enjoyed the voyage from Bristol to Barbados on the s.s. *Inanda*. He participated in the playing of harmless pranks, another less remembered side of his character as a young man. He became a member of the team's impromptu jazz orchestra which accompanied dancing on board ship and was subsequently asked to perform in Trinidad. His own instrument was the flexitone, made from bent steel. His contribution appealed to the West Indians.

His 238 not out in the first representative game against the West Indies (not yet a Test side) was then the highest made in the Caribbean by an MCC player. From that game at Barbados, the party sailed for Trinidad where Hammond played against Learie Constantine for the first time. In the colony game in Trinidad each man took the other's wicket.

Hammond and Constantine would meet each other over the next 20 years. They were very close in age and each had an ability that marked him out from his fellow-players. In cricketing terms there was much common ground. They were among the outstanding fielders of their generation, both were all-rounders and either man had it in him to turn a match by an individual performance. Each could command the devotion of the cricket-loving public. Both liked to bowl with their caps on. Between the two there existed some rivalry. Constantine for some years nursed the feeling that Hammond had slighted him when he arrived in Trinidad. Hammond's reserved nature, except perhaps among those whom he really knew, could be taken amiss, especially by a sensitive young coloured player. The feeling, more on Constantine's part than Hammond's, led to some tension in the relatively few times the two players met on the field until it was resolved, as we shall see, at Old Trafford in 1933. During the war they were opposing captains and Hammond declared that the West Indies 'could not have had a better captain or a more inspiring player to lead them.' As late as 1954, when Constantine successfully applied for the post of assistant legal adviser to Trinidad Leaseholds Ltd, Hammond was one of his referees and wrote personally to his own friend, Simon Vos, the Company's chairman.

Hammond's bowling in the match against Trinidad, at a great pace on the matting wicket, led to his opening the bowling in the second representative match against the West Indies. From Trinidad the party went to the steaming tropical heat of British Guiana where he made a century against the colony. The match had sad consequences for him. He was stung by a mosquito and the infection lingered. The long journey by ship from British Guiana to Jamaica was passed in great pain. He played against Jamaica, bowled 25 overs and made a few runs but the poison grew worse. In the days before antibiotics, life and limb were much more easily at risk from such incidents.

The trip which had begun so light-heartedly – 'when not playing cricket we were free to behave like cheerful holiday-makers' – ended in sadness. He sailed home with MCC in a ship too small to carry a doctor and went straight to hospital in Bristol where he remained for some months. For a time his life hung in the balance and surgeons contemplated amputating his leg. The plea of his mother that this would end his livelihood led them to do all they could to avoid taking such a drastic step. In the end both Hammond's leg and his life were saved.

Among those who visited him was P. F. Warner who, as we have seen, had assessed Hammond's abilities very early on. He assured the sick man that he had a great future. Warner was chairman of the selectors. The England side regained the Ashes that summer with a side which, in Warner's words, 'would have been a great one' if Hammond had been available for it.

Hammond for his part recorded his own recollections of that sick-bed visit. Warner 'gave me the strength to turn the dark corner from hopelessness back to life.' By September 1926, he could turn up at Folkestone to watch a side of his colleagues on the West Indies tour play Kent in the Festival.

Thus a friendship began between the two men that lasted over the years. Warner, 30 years Hammond's senior, had the highest regard for him as a cricketer. It was he who, as chairman of the selectors in 1938, appointed him England captain. Warner was also among the few in the cricket world who got to know Hammond really well and who broke through the barriers of shyness and reserve. Years later, Warner wrote of Hammond as 'reliable, sensible and a good companion. Success did not spoil him in the least. On the contrary, as his fame grew, the more modest he became.' Curiously, the same sentiments had been expressed by a journalist writing in the *All Sports Weekly* just before Hammond went off to the West Indies. He described him as 'agreeable and companionable' and apt to be depressed after a run of bad luck, with the fear that he would never make runs again. Muriel Pannell and her family knew this. They had observed, at very close quarters during the past few years, a shy, handsome young man, a little lonely, very uncertain of himself, responsive only to people he was sure of. Their successive homes in Southsea, Waterlooville and later in Winchester were havens to which Walter Hammond would thankfully retreat from the ever-increasing publicity which came his way in the inter-war years.

As for Gloucestershire, his fellow-players had come to accept the young man who, in those days of acute social distinctions, seemed to fall between the gentlemen-amateurs and the playing professionals. He was a product neither of the public schools and Oxbridge nor of an all-age elementary school. In the pre-1926 Gloucestershire side he had no particular friends except for Neale and it may be that his habit of making most of his friendships outside the game was formed in those years.

3

England Cricketer, 1926–29

'The possibilities of this boy Hammond are beyond the scope of estimation'.
Illustrated Sporting News, 1927

In the early afternoon of the last Saturday in May 1927, the spectators at Southampton enjoyed the spectacle of an off-drive for six which took Hammond's score to 114. They were witnesses of his thirteenth century in first-class cricket and the occasion had its own vintage quality. But for those who followed the game, and especially for Hammond himself, the vintage had especial value. Eight months earlier, in that same port of Southampton, he had climbed awkwardly with the aid of two sticks up the gangway of the Castle liner bound for South Africa, a pale and shrunken young man seeking sunshine and health.

Gloucestershire, deprived of Hammond's services throughout 1926 and falling to third from bottom of the Championship table, were determined to have him fit for 1927 and sent him to South Africa to recover his health. With his arrival began an association with a country in which he would eventually live. He spent the South African summer with the Green Point Club in Cape Town, coaching, playing and getting well. He looked back on it as one of the pleasantest periods of his life. He always thrived on sunshine, and sport in any guise appealed. Swimming and tennis wrought a cure and by May 1927 he was back in England ready to pick up the threads of his career. He was still only 23. In two years' time he would return to England from Australia as the principal celebrity

in a successful team and with claims to being the greatest cricketer
in the world. Cricket was to be his entire life for the next two years,
and he would not see another English winter's day until the end of
1929.

But such triumphs had to be wrested from stern reality and the
pursuit of them began in 1927 on the Wagon Works ground at
Gloucester where he made a century in the opening game. Two
days later he made a century in each innings against Surrey. Since
Gloucestershire followed on, he batted twice with only minutes
separating the two occasions. That performance was dwarfed at
Old Trafford. Out for 99, 'being careless', he ruefully wrote, he
made 187 runs in the second innings. All were agreed that his batting was one of the greatest displays seen there for many years. He
hooked McDonald with a force that caused the ball to scatter the
grit and pebbles beyond the grass. He had shown, said *The Times*,
as had great batsmen of the past, 'that a man who will go out for his
strokes will make runs'.

Cardus was there to record the occasion for his *Manchester
Guardian* readers the next morning:

> It was one of the greatest innings ever witnessed on the ground. No
> other living Englishman could have given us cricket so full of mingled
> style and power, an innings of strength, bravery, sweetness and light.
> Not an ounce of power seemed to go to waste. Art directed the driving
> force of it all.

A few days later he returned to the 'grandeur' of Hammond's
batting in an article in the *Illustrated Sporting News*:

> If I sit down, close my eyes, and think of all the glorious batsmanship
> I have ever seen – even then the bloom and power of Hammond's
> innings remain warmly and incomparably in my mind. The possi-
> bilities of this boy Hammond are beyond the scope of estimation; I
> tremble with delight at the very thought of the grandeur he will spread
> over our cricket fields when he has come to maturity. He is, in his own
> way, another Trumper in the making. His innings against Lancashire
> satisfied every reasonable ideal of the great batsman. In an hour the
> Lancashire bowling was routed, and the Lancashire crowd was sent half
> crazy by the beauty and bravery of the cricket.

In 13 days Hammond had amassed 712 runs. As he drove to play
Leicestershire he realised that he was three-quarters of the way

to equalling Grace's feat of 1000 runs in May. Only twice had 1000 runs been scored by 31 May: Grace had done so in 1895 and the Surrey batsman, Tom Hayward, in 1900. If Hammond had realised, so had the press! Even in an age less conscious of the media, the public were alerted to the prospect and the gate, that Saturday at Hinckley, was considerably up on Leicestershire's usual expectations

The bat with which he had made those runs at Old Trafford happened to be in the pavilion at Hinckley. A Leicestershire member who examined it wrote to me saying that there was not a mark within one inch of either edge. That supporter felt his whole day was ruined when George Geary dismissed Hammond for 4. Hammond had already acquired the quality of being a greater attraction than the contest. Cardus had noted it in a Lancashire patriot in the previous game who remarked, ''opes he gets couple 'undred.' To Cardus's comment, 'What about Lancashire?' he had replied, 'Lancashire be blowed. I was born at Throstle's Nest alright but . . . oh, well hit, sir!'

His next chance came before his own home crowd at Bristol against Middlesex. Gloucestershire were badly beaten by an innings despite Hammond's 83 which was entirely within the mood of his batting that month and took him to within 114 of his target. So he came to that last Saturday in May against Hampshire at Southampton. A large crowd had turned out in the hope of seeing history being made and they were not disappointed. Gloucestershire won the toss and shortly before lunch, Hammond was at the wicket. An hour and a half later came the one hundredth and fourteenth run which equalled Grace's record of 1000 runs in May. Eventually he was out for 192.

On the Monday he was the subject of the *Manchester Guardian*'s leading article. We may make a reasonable guess at the authorship! Hammond was called 'one of the most chivalrous of batsmen' and he shared the day's news with the visit of the American transatlantic pilot, Colonel Charles Lindbergh, to Britain. They were two heroes.

The return to Bristol was a Roman triumph not without its dinares to the tune of £300 and a gold watch and chain raised from a 'shilling fund' opened by the *Bristol Times*. For their generosity, he rewarded his own Bristol supporters with three centuries in a week. Nearby Taunton saw a score of 197 against Somerset and only a spell of rain late in the month prevented his adding a further 1000 in June. Meanwhile, he had been selected for the South against the North in a Test trial at Bramall Lane, Sheffield.

Test trials were the public's consolation for there being no Test matches in 1927. The New Zealanders were paying their first visit but their elevation to Test status lay in the future. A second Test trial in July was played at Bristol, and Gloucestershire supporters were able to see Hammond playing for 'England' for the first time, coming in fourth after Hobbs, Sutcliffe and Charles Hallows had collected some 300 runs first.

Hammond ended the season, the first at home in which he had established himself without question as a front-rank English cricketer, by playing for the MCC South African XI at Scarborough. The invitation to play meant, of course, that he was one of the party who would sail for South Africa in a few days. It was the appropriate reward for his summer's endeavour. He had scored 2969 runs, made a dozen centuries, and lay fifth in the national batting averages.

Wisden featured him in the 'Five Cricketers of the Year', curiously portraying him in a well-cut three-piece suit. In summing up his achievements, the writer concluded:

> Beautifully built and loose limbed with strong and pliant wrists, Hammond is essentially a stylist in method, and moreover, a firm believer in making the bat hit the ball. For the most part he is a forward player, and even in making a defensive stroke in this way he comes down harder on the ball than does the average man. He employs all the modern means of scoring, and can cut and turn the ball to leg with equal skill, but, above everything else, his driving is superb. With a new ball he can be most deceptive with his medium pace bowling, obtaining swerve in flight, and imparting spin to get life off the pitch. A beautiful fielder he is particularly brilliant in the slips or anywhere on the off-side.

It may serve as a contemporary judgement of his technique as he entered the great years of his career. Elsewhere in *Wisden*, the Gloucestershire county report highlighted a weakness in the county from which Hammond cannot be entirely disassociated. That weakness was the lack of bowlers. Not one recruit of real ability had been discovered since the war to give support to Parker. Tom Goddard's great successes still lay in the future. Hammond, in a summer in which his batting average of 72.00 eclipsed anything in modern Gloucestershire history, had taken only 16 wickets at a cost of 44. There were those who were content it should be so. That Hammond should not be made into an all-rounder had been the plea, as we have seen, of one commentator before he went to the West Indies. Yet in the view of many, he had it in him to be a great medium-fast bowler. Gloucestershire did not press the point. He never joined the ranks of those all-rounders who got their 1000 runs and 100 wickets a summer and his own reluctance to be as good a bowler as he might have been must be seen as the main cause.

The side which sailed for South Africa in September 1927 was by no means fully representative of contemporary English cricket since players of the calibre of Hobbs, Hendren and Maurice Tate were not available. But a party which included Sutcliffe, R. E. S. Wyatt, E. R. T. Holmes, Tyldesley and Hammond as batsmen and Geary, S. J. Staples and A. P. Freeman as bowlers was still believed to be strong enough to meet the South Africans. In the event, Geary broke down, the series was drawn, and Hammond had to perform as an all-rounder.

So it came about that on Christmas Eve 1927 at Johannesburg, in the hundred and fifty-first first-class match of his career, W. R. Hammond made his Test debut, nearly 7½ years after his debut at Cheltenham. Many a less distinguished cricketer has waited fewer years. Yet Hammond was still only 24 and Test matches were infrequent in his younger days. Indeed, only 25 had been played by England since the first world war.

Hammond had waited all those years to play for England. Yet his captain in that Test, R. T. Stanyforth, was also playing in his first Test with a cricket background that included no first-class county affiliation. It was still an age when amateurs and professionals in the game came from very different stables. Hammond's first Test brought him a half-century and an analysis of 5 for 36 in the second innings. The series in particular and the tour as a whole did not offer quite the success which events of the previous summer had suggested. Only the East London spectators saw him at his very best when he made 166 not out against Border. Yet 908 runs in all and 15 Test wickets (no-one took more) was no mean return. He had let South Africa off lightly in 1927–28. He would be back!

The summer of 1928 was one he gave to Gloucestershire rather than to England. In the three Test matches against the West Indies he had a top score of 63. For Gloucestershire he topped both batting and bowling averages and took 58 catches. He made three double-centuries and a spectacular 166 at Lord's in a game in which his bowling and catching were almost as important.

Indeed, the standard he set in the field raised the whole Gloucestershire XI so that there were, *Wisden* commented, 'days when catches of outstanding brilliance marked the play of the team.' His bowling was extremely effective and he and the other all-rounder, Reg Sinfield, gave the support which Parker so much needed. Gloucestershire, for the first time since the war, were in contention for the Championship. In the end they were fifth, a result which pleased and brought in the crowds.

The crowds who flocked to the Cheltenham Festival, one of the gracious occasions in the English cricket calendar, saw him at his finest. In the Surrey match he scored a century in each innings separated by a performance in the field in which he had opened the bowling, secured the wicket of Hobbs and taken four catches. Surrey were set 357 to win. He secured a further six catches, five of them off Parker's bowling, and his aggregate of ten catches ranked as a record for a non-wicket-keeper.

The Cheltenham Festival crowds whose cup was full that August Friday afternoon returned in the morning to witness a spectacular bowling performance. The pitch had early-morning dew which he used to advantage. In scarcely more than an hour Worcestershire were back in the pavilion. Hammond had taken 9 for 23 in ten overs and caught the tenth man off Parker's bowling. By mid-afternoon he was at the wicket, contributing 80 runs to a huge Gloucestershire lead.

The Festival, Gloucestershire's home programme and Hammond's spectacular *tour de force* concluded on the Monday when he and Parker each bowled 33 overs unchanged to defeat Worcestershire by an innings. Hammond's 6 for 105 brought his match aggregate to 15. In the two games he had made over 360 runs and taken 16 wickets and 11 catches. It was an all-round performance unparalleled before or since.

The serious business of the season was done. There were other Festival matches and the boat to catch to Australia. He had made 2825 runs for an average of 65.69.

Yet, attractive as run-making is to spectators and to statisticians, perhaps too many runs had been made in 1928. Five men, for example, topped the 3000 in 1928 (and Hammond was not among them) while only ten had done so previously in the whole history of the game. The editor of *Wisden* gave the matter an airing:

'Those responsible for the control of the game are faced – to a greater degree than ever before – with the difficulty of reducing run-getting to reasonable limits.' Among solutions proposed was a change in the lbw rule, higher stumps and less well-dressed wickets. Hammond also became convinced in the 1930s that batsmen were making too many runs.

The side which went to Australia in September 1928 under A. P. F. Chapman was, as one of its few survivors told me and as the journalist S. J. Southerton confirmed at the time, a team who went through the tour 'with splendid harmony prevailing all the time'. The advantages, from a technical point of view, were theirs from the start. They were the holders of the Ashes, won at the Oval in 1926. They included cricketers of outstanding merit. They were led by a captain whose own fielding was an inspiration and whose leadership was tactically of high quality. Hammond himself felt that Chapman had the right temperament for Australia – 'sanguine, happy, eager; he made friends everywhere and no-one in or out of the team could resist his cheery good-nature.'

On such firm foundations was success built up. The team 'both on and off the field left an extremely favourable impression wherever they went,' Southerton recorded. 'A happy family off the field, they pulled together in every match like a well-oiled machine.'

In the view of the manager of the tour, Frederick Toone, knighted after the tour, players were chosen with more than their cricketing qualities borne in mind. In words which have an archaic ring 50 years later, they had to be 'of good character, high principle, easy of address and in every personal sense worthy of representing their country irrespective of their work on the field.' The enterprise, concluded Toone, was 'imperial' and 'the spirit of imperialism which animated the party had a very ready response from the Australian public at large.'

To the cricketers themselves the essence of this imperial adventure was a martial one. A campaign had to be won and no amount of abstract language could disguise the fact that victory was sweeter than defeat; that the Ashes had to be retained; that the rubber fought out on the four great grounds of Australia mattered before all else; that the weary travellers, some 50,000 miles and six months later, would arrive at Victoria Station to be either lauded as victors or shrugged off as vanquished. Yet the philosophy which Toone upheld proved important. In the harmony of 1928–29 were laid the foundations which allowed England and Australia to survive the discords of the next tour four years later.

In the early weeks of the tour Hammond made a century against South Australia and a double-century against New South Wales. That innings at Sydney was described as 'a perfect exhibition' but was modestly written off by himself as an innings in which all he had to do was take care 'and knock up the runs'. His modesty about his own performances was an attractive trait he never lost. It helps to explain why he was sometimes reluctant to praise the performance of others. He simply could not see what the fuss was about! The 'fuss' was enshrined for ever in Herbert Fishwick's famous photograph of him driving into the covers and taken during that game (photo no. 8).

The match at Sydney had its own special appeal. It was the first time Hammond had played against Don Bradman. Bradman's reply to Hammond's double-century was to make 87 and 132 not out. It was too early to talk about rivalry and the Test series which followed belonged indisputably to Hammond. But Bradman was in the wings. Soon, very soon, he would challenge Hammond's achievements.

Meanwhile, Hammond was continuing to fulfil all the expectations save one. He had yet to make a century in a Test. That omission he rectified in his tenth appearance for England in the second Test at Sydney. England compiled 636, every man making double figures, and Hammond amassed 251. It was an innings which lasted from just after lunch on the second day until one o'clock on the fourth. Only R. E. Foster's 287 on the same ground in 1905 had eclipsed it in Test matches. Percy Fender, who some had hoped would have been the England captain, reported the tour instead:

Hammond's innings was a classic. He attacked the bowling all the time except during the last 23 balls he received. He stood back on his right foot and made that wristy drive into the covers continually until the ball was pitched a little farther up, when he occasionally went out and drove it. None of the bowlers was able to keep him quiet and cover fielders were literally bombarded. His timing was perfect. Except for the fine work done in the cover positions, he would have made many more runs.

The *Sydney Morning Herald* declared:

Figures cannot convey the charm and variety of his strokes. It is doubt-
ful if there is a player in the world from whom the ball travels with
more pace.

His performance won him a 'shilling fund' collection organised
by the *Sydney Sun*. He was grateful for the generosity of the
Australian public, who were conscious that English professional
cricketers did not earn large sums. Top English cricketers were
beginning to be aware of their commercial potential, but the days
of Kerry Packer lay far in the future.

A few days later, at Melbourne, he scored another double-
century in the third Test and added two more centuries in his two
innings in the fourth Test. Of them all, his 177 in the second
innings of the fourth Test was rated the best. After a partnership of
262 with Jardine no-one else stayed for any length. His innings of
seven hours made possible an England victory by 12 runs, a
narrow margin compared with those by which England had won
all the three previous Tests.

The 903 runs Hammond made in the series exceeded all
records. His average was over 100. In the tour as a whole he made
over 1500 runs for an average of 91. No-one else came near. He
was, wrote M. A. Noble, the former Australian captain, 'the sheet-
anchor of the side, a truly great all-rounder'. Despite the 'arrival'
of Bradman, Hammond's performance led Noble to pose the
question, 'Can we [Australians] view the future with equanimity or
any degree of confidence?'

During that long tour, Hammond shed the last of his youth. The
responsibilities of his major role as the principal run-getter, and as
a supporting bowler good enough to dismiss W. M. Woodfull,
strengthened that part of his character which was by nature
serious. The change which came over him as a cricketer matched
him as a man. The cricket required, as Cardus observed, that the
impulsive, dashing, front-foot player, became the 'batsman of
rational poise who played henceforth from the back foot' when
circumstance demanded. He became much more a rational man.
Emotion lay concealed. Friendships were not easily won. In that
cheerful touring party he was on the edge of the group, something
of a 'loner', cautiously establishing an acquaintance with Leslie
Ames which would blossom into friendship on the next tour of
Australia.

But the Australian public acclaimed him. They had just bidden farewell to their own great men of the early 1920s; Bardsley and Macartney had gone from the scene. The Australian girls fell for the aquiline ruggedness of the 25-year-old Englishman who was always immaculately turned-out and well-groomed. Some pestered him with letters. A few of them he wined and dined. Although most were left to adore from a distance, Hammond now and later found himself more at ease with the opposite sex than with his own.

The playwright, Ben Travers, a life-long devotee of cricket, accompanied the MCC party for a large part of the tour. He was an acute observer of the game and Hammond appreciated the older man's judgement. Travers always felt he made him welcome. Perhaps there was an extra reason. Travers had an exceptionally fine pair of field-glasses and he recalled Hammond borrowing them during the Sydney Test with the object of examining at closer quarters the many attractive ladies sitting in the enclosure. Travers got his glasses back with a laconic comment and the two men resumed their study of the play.

Hammond had left for Australia on the threshold of greatness and returned having crossed it. The crowds who mobbed the MCC party on their arrival at Victoria Station could scarcely be contained by a cordon of police, four-deep. They acclaimed everyone but most of all Wally Hammond. The English cricketing public was ready to look for a new hero as Hobbs began a gentle descent from the highest pinnacles of achievement and veneration. That hero would be Hammond. For the next ten years what he did was a matter of popular concern. He offered to cricket in particular a subject for technical admiration and statistical appraisal. He presented to a much larger and less definable cricketing following something positive in the negative years of the Depression, a focal point for all that was English when rumours of war threatened that inheritance. He provided for all men a conversation-piece.

4
The Great All-Rounder, 1929–32

'The best all-round player in the world'.
The *Daily Mail*, 1932

A few days after arriving in England, Hammond went north to Yorkshire to marry Dorothy Lister, daughter of Joseph Lister, a Bradford textile merchant. The couple had met eighteen months earlier at the 1927 Scarborough Festival, when both Dorothy and her sister had been his dancing partners in the evenings.

The wedding took place on 24 April 1929 in Bingley Parish Church and was conducted by the Bishop of Bradford. The Listers were people of substance in Yorkshire and the occasion was one of importance. Mills and shops were closed for the day. 'Mill girls with shawls over their heads and fashionable ladies thronged the church,' said the local paper. It was a full three hours before the service. Roads into Bingley were blocked and traffic, in those days of fewer cars, had to be controlled by extra police. Pathé Newsreel men recorded the scene for the nation to see on its cinema screens.

Two hundred guests went to the reception at the Masonic Hall, where the cake was crowned with a replica of the Ashes. Hammond's best man was Henry Pannell and Herbert Sutcliffe was an usher. Distinguished cricketers mixed with Yorkshire business folk. Someone remarked to their neighbour that it was a union of 'fame and brass'. The comment was apt. Hammond was certainly the man of the hour in 1929 and Dorothy's family were able to give the couple a financial start which enabled them to purchase a home. Among their presents was a silver cigar-box presented from the 1928–29 MCC side which is now a collector's piece, attracting a buyer at an auction in the late 1970s. Gloucestershire County Cricket Club gave them a wedding present of 50 guineas which appeared on the audited accounts for 1929. As a measure of Hammond's value to Gloucestershire, it represented a seventh of the secretary's annual salary and more than twice the county telephone bill for the entire year. A further £50 went through the books from collections through the local press.

There was a very brief honeymoon on the Continent before the couple moved into a new bungalow, in Sixty Acres, Failand, just across the county border in Somerset. They called their house 'Westholme' and they possessed the unusual telephone number of the single digit, 7.

Dorothy Lister found herself in a new world. She had never travelled beyond Yorkshire and her life had been bound up in the small industrial town where she had grown up. Events had centred round her family, which she had been used to having around her, and the ties were close. She was one of a set of young people, the children of wealthy parents, whose social life involved them in dances and parties in the county. These were the 1920s, the years of escapism and the Charleston.

To the newness and strangeness which married life brought was added the loneliness of the cricket 'widow'. Dorothy was quickly made to realise what life was like for a professional cricketer's wife. Her husband, within a day or two of their return, went to Birmingham where Gloucestershire began their 1929 season. Six weeks after his last innings of 80 at Perth, he took 238 not out off the Warwickshire attack. 'Tiger' Smith, the Warwickshire wicket-keeper, remembered the ferocity of his off-driving, a quality of batsmanship which another opponent that day, Jack Parsons, also displayed.

From Edgbaston, Hammond went to Leyton where he entertained the Essex crowd in their first match with another century. That was in the first innings. On the last day of the game he took delivery of a Saloon Graham Paige, thus becoming the first professional cricketer to be given a sponsored car. The driver bringing it down had hoped to see him bat and spend the day at Leyton but, on hearing Hammond's laconic comment 'In, out, duck', had no excuse for staying. Next on this southern tour, Gloucestershire opened Sussex's home programme at Brighton. Then it was time to go home, play at Bristol and make a start in married life at Sixty Acres. There the Hammonds lived until the outbreak of the second world war ten years later.

The fortunes of Gloucestershire prospered in 1929. They were in the running for the Championship until mid-August but defeat by Sussex by a single run and by Notts by an innings left them fourth in the final placing. By the standards Hammond set himself (or others expected of him) he did not perform quite so out-standingly as a batsman, though many a cricketer would have settled for even a portion of his average of 66.53. As a bowler, he was sparingly in demand with the emergence of Tom Goddard as a major spearhead in the attack. It became Gloucestershire's practice to open with a few overs from Sinfield and Charles Barnett and then bring on Parker and Goddard.

Again the county had an outstanding fielding side under the inspiration of both B. H. Lyon, the new captain, and Hammond himself. Lyon, in Hammond's own view, 'galvanized Gloucester-shire cricket. He had a way of keeping everyone on their toes even in the longest or most quiet spell of play.' Under Lyon, they set their cap at the Championship with a policy of going all out for victory. As a consequence no county won as many matches, but sometimes the gamble failed and Gloucestershire lost games which might have been saved.

The South Africans were visiting England. Hammond appeared in four of the five Tests, missing one through injury. He scored centuries at Edgbaston and the Oval. The first hundred had all the characteristics of his recent Australian form. The second, when no result was in sight, involved him in a huge partnership with Sutcliffe who became the first man to make two hundreds in a Test on two occasions.

Towards the end of August, Dorothy joined the Pannells and her mother-in-law for a holiday in the Isle of Wight. An injured knee released her husband from the last few county games and he was able to join her.

Gloucestershire renewed their bid for the title in 1930. Again 15 matches were won, again these were more than any other county, again the side owed a great deal to Lyon's leadership, again Hammond topped the averages. The season finished in a tremendous struggle, Gloucestershire winning seven out of their last eight county matches to finish second in the table behind Lancashire. Hammond's contribution included a century against

Somerset and a bowling performance against Glamorgan in which he took 12 for 74. Both these successes were on the Clifton College ground and were remembered with affection by fellow-Clifton residents who had known him in his bachelor days there and remained loyal supporters when he played on the local ground.

The Championship aside, Gloucestershire played a memorable game against the Australians. The tourists had had a successful summer in which the English debut of Bradman established his greatness and the Australians wrought their revenge for 1928–29 by winning the Ashes. It was a series of massive scoring in which England came off second-best. Comparing some of the first innings totals in the Tests makes the point – 425 to 729; 391 to 566; 251 to 345; 405 to 695. Those huge Australian totals owed most to Bradman's 254, 334, 14 and 232. Figures of such proportions were to be the hallmark of Bradman's career. Statistically he averaged 139.14 (without a 'not out' to help) in that series. When he finally retired from Test cricket in 1948, 0.06 separated him from an overall career Test average of 100 – just four more runs were needed!

The advent of Bradman meant that Hammond had met his equal as an accumulator of runs. Up to a point, their respective performances determined the outcome of the Anglo-Australian series for the next 17 years. When Bradman imposed, Australia won. If Hammond dictated, England were victorious.

In 1930 it was Bradman who prevailed and Hammond had to settle for some 300 runs in nine innings. Of himself he said, 'I was not very satisfied with my results,' and of his rival, 'He will long remain the true pattern of a modern batsman.' What had temporarily brought Hammond to ground was the leg-break bowling of C. V. Grimmett who, in a wet summer, dismissed Hammond on five occasions. And Grimmett's bowling brings us to that match between Gloucestershire and the Australians at Bristol.

Playing near enough the side which had triumphed at the Oval at four o'clock the previous afternoon, the tourists put Gloucestershire in to bat. In 2¼ hours on a wet wicket the county were bowled out for 72. Grimmett and P. M. Hornibrook picked up the wickets, Hammond staying an hour for 17. Of Grimmett's bowling he wrote:

Those slow leg-breaks of his, almost round-arm, with the ball curling in towards the batsman as if answering to some powerful magnet,

were helped by the damp, heavy, air. When you felt you were beginning to get the hang of them, he would put down a wicked top-spinner
or a selection of unplayable googlies.

The Australians responded with 157, finding in Goddard an
outstanding bowler whom they had seen in only one Test.
Gloucestershire in their second innings reached 202, an overall
lead of 117. Hammond's own share was 89 runs in an innings he
vividly described:

> It is not vanity, I hope, to say that I realized that much depended on my
> innings. It was obvious, at any rate, that the Australians thought so. Not
> even in many Test innings have I been flattered with such unflinching
> attention, or so many and such wicked traps. Eleven men willed me not
> to run – or, if I ran, to run myself out. One bowler after another sent me
> down balls that offered nothing whatever except dismissal. I scored a
> few runs. After what seemed a lifetime, I got into double figures.
>
> I knew I must 'farm' Grimmett as much as I could. I had to keep the
> strike so as to play my partners in. The innings developed something of
> the quality of a nightmare. I heard a lot of clapping, and saw that I had
> got 50. I stopped to wipe the perspiration that was threatening to get
> into my eyes and spoil my sight of the ball, or to loose my grip on the
> handle of an old and loved bat.
>
> I got 89. They got me then, and it says something for the excitement
> of the game that it was not till I was in the pavilion that I felt disappoint-
> ment at not getting my century.

Wisden commented that Hammond's innings was 'faultless'. After
he had gone Gloucestershire's last wickets fell for 36.

The Australians, needing 118, reached 50 without loss but a
collapse after lunch on the last day suddenly made everyone aware
of a tremendous finish. By now the excitement had spread through
the city. 17,000 people crowded the ground and the gates were
closed for the first time since 1888. Five wickets were down with
the total at 73. Eight runs later Parker bowled Bradman. With the
match going Gloucestershire's way, Grimmett took command –
with the bat. The Australians crept up to 106 for 8 and then, with
Grimmett's dismissal to 115 for 9. There came two singles and,
with the scores level, 18 balls were bowled without a run. Finally
an lbw appeal went Goddard's way and the match had ended in a
tie.

Hammond called it 'the most exciting game of my life'. This

normally reserved, unemotional cricketer was carried away by the occasion. He described the last ball of the match – and its aftermath:

'How wuz her, then?'
   Tom's familiar yell follows the clip of the ball on Hornibrook's pad as part of the same sound. Then – the umpire's finger goes up. . . .
   Pandemonium breaks loose! A tie! The crowd comes onto the grass as if the walls of a dam had burst. Above the great surge of dark clothes froths a white foam of hands and programmes. We are inundated. Players are slung up onto shoulders with as little care as sacks of wheat. A continuous deafening shouting stupefies the senses, and a thousand hands beat our backs and wring our arms almost from their sockets.
   Somehow we have to get to the station to catch the train for Swansea. I do not know how it was done. All I remember is a vast confusion, and my aching back and arms. The approach to the station, the booking office, the platforms, seethed and thundered with hilarious mobs, shouting, singing and yelling.

The scores of the game were printed in gold on silk and presented to the players. One of them, Reg Sinfield, recalled the game to me 50 years later and proudly displayed his copy of that scoresheet framed in a place of honour in his house. He had, he said, 'never seen Wally so excited'.

Gloucestershire made a third challenging bid for the title in 1931, finishing second but far behind Yorkshire. Lyon's pursuit of the title, in this his last regular year as captain, was unavailing, but his side still set the standard in fielding. Hammond, in particular, performed miracles at second slip. Of his five centuries, that against Sussex at Brighton was the most spectacular, his score advancing from 118 to 168 in a little over 20 minutes. Overall, he made far fewer runs than his supporters expected, although he remained the mainstay of the batting.

In the intervening winter of 1930–31 he had again toured South Africa. Chapman captained a side which did not quite reflect the contemporary strength of English cricket and, in the event, the rubber was lost. South Africa won the first Test, the only one in which a conclusion was reached. Hammond proved the most successful batsman on both matting and turf wickets and topped the averages. He could nearly always be depended on to score over 50. In the second, third and fifth Tests he opened the batting with Wyatt and their start was always sound.

He was a man for whom cricketing tours were a chance to see the world as well as play cricket. He took advantage of a few days in Rhodesia, when illness caused him to retire from the match against the colony, to visit the Victoria Falls, 'a roar like one unending and undying roll of the loudest thunder you ever heard,' he wrote. On his return to England in 1931, in the three-match, rain-affected, series with New Zealand he scored a century at the Oval 'with such skill and power that not one of the bowlers could keep a length'.

The fortunes of Gloucestershire declined in 1932. Among reasons for this decline were the falling in standards of the two stalwarts of the side, Parker and Dipper, and the absence of Harry Smith, a wicket-keeper capable of taking the bowling of both Parker and Goddard. But another perceptible reason was a change in captaincy. Lyon was unable to play regularly and Hammond was appointed vice-captain. Hammond was conscious of Lyon's mantle and he commented that 'the breathtaking risks [Lyon] had taken, and won so many victories with, were not for any beginner in the art of captaincy to take. On the other hand, it was naturally expected of me that I should not lose the keen public support that Lyon's attractive leadership had won us.'

His own evaluation fits in with the more objective comment of others. H. E. Roslyn, for long *Wisden*'s Gloucestershire correspondent, stated that he 'often showed shrewdness and judgement but there were occasions when he failed to inspire his colleagues to put forth the little extra needed to force a win.' In one match, for example, against Glamorgan at Swansea, a good declaration by Hammond was followed by some uncertain leadership in the field, allowing Glamorgan to scrape home in a game which Gloucestershire might have won.

One accusation which critics of Hammond's captaincy could not make against him was that of selfishness. Twice he declared the innings closed when near to his own century in an effort to produce a result. Sinfield recalled batting with him at Northampton and both of them scoring freely. The New Zealander, C. C. Dacre, replaced Sinfield and the runs continued to come quickly. With a whole day's play left to dismiss Northamptonshire, Hammond declared when he was 92, 'although we urged him to get the last eight he needed first'. Wally Hammond never thought himself greater than the game.

Yet great he was, in that summer of 1932. He continued to dominate the English scene and make a spectacular contribution.

The brief experiment in captaincy was not continued and an assessment of his role in that department must await a later chapter. He made over 2500 runs and took over 50 wickets. He made twice as many runs and twice as many centuries as anyone else in the Gloucestershire side and his average was, at 60, twice as high. His then highest score in his career came against Lancashire at Liverpool. Sinfield and Barnett had given Gloucestershire a very good start, whereupon Hammond scored 264 out of the next 409 runs. His immense stamina was once again illustrated. He was on the field all but 90 minutes of the three-day game, batted for over six hours and bowled 77 overs in the two consecutive Lancashire innings, virtually without a rest, taking seven wickets. Lancashire must have had enough of him that summer. Ten days earlier he had made 164 and 48 against them at the Cheltenham Festival and led his side to victory.

He chose the classic fixture of those days, Gentlemen v. Players at Lord's, to rectify a personal omission – a century in that game. Befittingly, it was done in the grand manner in the highest company. The pressmen jostled for eulogies. The hundreds made by Hobbs, K. S. Duleepsinhji and the Nawab of Pataudi in the same game did nothing to diminish that of Hammond. Great as they all were, said the critics, Hammond overshadowed everything. He was, said the *Daily Mail*, 'the best all-round player in the world and possibly bracketed equally with Bradman as the best batsman'. A few months earlier Bradman had been warming up for the next encounter with England by averaging over 200 against the South Africans.

That encounter proved to be the notorious bodyline tour of 1932–33 in which England won the series by four Tests to one. A party of very considerable talent under the leadership of Jardine amassed totals of over 500 four times before Christmas, beating three of the States by an innings and winning the first Test match. All this was accomplished (besides losing the second Test) before the storm broke in mid-January. A sequence of cables was exchanged which nearly brought the series to a close and threatened diplomatic relations between the two countries. A year before, the Statute of Westminster (1931) had increased Australian independence of English law. The measure, principally of interest to politicians, lawyers and academics, nevertheless reflected Australia's strong sense of nationalism. Furthermore, there was Australian discontent at British policy over the conversion of

some Treasury Bonds, so the contests with England had something more to them than just displays of cricketing skills.

This book cannot be concerned with the detailed issues of the
bodyline debate. Indeed, within a few months of the tour, the
editor of *Wisden* could write, 'Happily the controversy is at an end,
and little reason exists, therefore, to flog what we can regard as a
"dead horse".' Hammond was neither a major bowler in the Test
series nor was he the captain. As a co-opted selector, he was on the
periphery of decision-making but he was in no sense a policy-
maker.

The policies which determined the approach of the England
captain towards the best and most effective way to beat Australia
had been first devised at a pre-tour meeting in London. Jardine had
invited Harold Larwood, Bill Voce and the former England and
current Nottinghamshire captain, Arthur Carr, to meet him. As
Jardine saw it, the dismissal of an Australian side containing the
batting strength of Bradman, W. H. Ponsford and Woodfull called
for extraordinary tactics. The statistics of the 1930 series were fresh
in the mind. If a way could be found to direct the attack towards the
leg stump, such prolific scoring might be contained. If, added to
that, the pace of the Australian wickets could be harnessed to best
advantage and the ball bowled short, then wickets might be won.
Finally, if a leg-side field were set with eight men to catch the
ball from the involuntary stroke the batsman made, then that
possibility became a near-certainty. Such, in essence, was what
Jardine and his companions devised.

What made it different from the legitimate and historic tradition
of fast bowling attacking the leg stump and putting in an occasional
short ball for good measure was its ruthless efficiency matched by
a frequent delivery of short-pitched balls. What made it controversial was the physical damage it caused to batsmen who were
forced to put personal safety before playing cricket.

Someone else whom Jardine had consulted in England had
been the former Warwickshire and England fast bowler, F. R.
Foster, who had been so successful in Australia in the 1911–12
series. When Foster realised the implications of Jardine's visits to
him he issued a press statement declaring that he had no idea that
his advice 'would be used for bodyline bowling. I would like all my
old friends in Australian cricket to know that I am sorry that my
experience and my advice were put to such unworthy uses.'

Hammond was aware of constant discussions on the trip out

between Jardine and his principal fast bowlers (a category in which Hammond could no longer genuinely claim to be) but he was not a participant. During subsequent events he was, as a member of the touring party, in no position to express a public view. Whatever the private feelings of himself and some others, such as the Nawab of Pataudi, were suspected to be, they outwardly accepted the cabled judgement of MCC that there was nothing unsportsmanlike about the policy being pursued.

Thirteen years later, on the eve of his departure to Australia as captain of the 1946–47 side, Hammond gave his views in an article in *The People*. It contained a rejection of bodyline bowling as he had seen it in 1932–33 and, to a lesser extent, from the West Indies in 1933. Bodyline bowling was an attack on the batsman which could only be avoided 'by risking serious injury or getting out quickly'. He believed only good luck had prevented anyone's death and he admitted that he would have got out of the game if such tactics had been persisted with.

He re-iterated these views in his book, *Cricket my Destiny*, published in 1946. He conceded that Jardine had some grounds for devising it if only to counter the constant negative play of the 1930 Australians in ignoring bowling outside the off stump. He believed that Jardine failed to anticipate the consequences of his actions in not realising how dangerous the bowling would be. He judged that Jardine got caught up in events. The more the Australian players – let alone the public – voiced their protests the more he was committed to persevere with it. To have done anything else would have been a withdrawal such as no captain, least of all a man of Jardine's autocratic nature, could have contemplated. Bradman believed that the Australian Board of Control should have spoken earlier after the second Test, which Australia won. He had no doubts that he himself was the principal target. Hammond went on to say that the only good which came out of the controversy was the change in Bradman's approach. No longer was Bradman the 'chanceless batsman'. Henceforth he responded to the abolition of bodyline by playing more attractively and 'accepting a more sporting sort of batting for his own'.

What Hammond wrote in public in 1946 he probably thought in private in 1933. The MCC party had maintained an outward show of loyalty to Jardine. There were four amateurs besides the captain and one professional, Sutcliffe, senior to Hammond. If it be a valid criticism that a collective stand should have been made

1 (above left). Hammond's father just before he was killed in action in France.

2 (above right). Hammond's mother: she was to outlive her son by five years.

3 (left). In Malta, aged 9.

4 (left). At Portsmouth Grammar School in the 3rd XI.

W.R. HAMMOND   P.G.S. 1916-18
AT HILSEA
LATER CAPTAIN OF GLOUCESTERSHIRE C.C.
AND ENGLAND

5 (below). At Cirencester Grammar School, fourth from the right in the back row.

6 (right). A snapshot taken by Grace James in 1925.

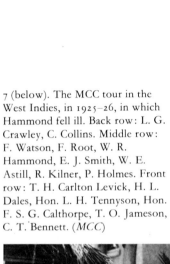

7 (below). The MCC tour in the West Indies, in 1925–26, in which Hammond fell ill. Back row: L. G. Crawley, C. Collins. Middle row: F. Watson, F. Root, W. R. Hammond, E. J. Smith, W. E. Astill, R. Kilner, P. Holmes. Front row: T. H. Carlton Levick, H. L. Dales, Hon. L. H. Tennyson, Hon. F. S. G. Calthorpe, T. O. Jameson, C. T. Bennett. (*MCC*)

8. The famous cover drive. This picture was taken in 1928 by the Sydney photographer, Herbert Fishwick, during the match against New South Wales and became the best-known picture of Hammond. Bertie Oldfield is keeping wicket. (*Sydney Morning Herald*)

9. The MCC tour in Australia, 1928–29, in which Hammond scored 903 runs in the Test series. Back row: G. Duckworth, L. E. G. Ames, C. P. Mead, M. W. Tate, E. H. Hendren, G. Geary. Middle row: M. Leyland, S. J. Staples, W. R. Hammond, F. C. Toone (manager), H. Sutcliffe, H. Larwood, A. P. Freeman. Front row: E. Tyldesley, J. C. White, A. P. F. Chapman, D. R. Jardine, J. B. Hobbs. (*MCC*)

10. 'He left for Australia on the threshold of greatness and returned having crossed it.' On the boat home, in 1929, hands in pockets in the back row. Also in the picture are George Duckworth, 'Patsy' Hendren and George Geary and (front row) Maurice Tate, C. P. Mead, J. C. White and Mr (later Sir Frederick) Toone, the manager. (*BBC Hulton Picture Library*)

11 (left). Going out to bat with B. H. Lyon for Gloucestershire against Essex in 1929. He made 127. (*BBC Hulton Picture Library*)

12 (below). A few days before this innings, he had married Dorothy Lister.

13. Batting at Leeds in the fourth Test against Australia, 1930. (*Press Association*)

14. Catching Don Bradman off Hedley Verity in a match against a Combined XI at Perth, 1932–33. Duckworth is keeping wicket. (*Illustrated London News*)

15. The Old Boys' match at Cirencester in 1935. Note the fashions of the pupils and Hammond's beloved hat.

16. Two years later, in 1937, Hammond began his association with Marsham Tyres. Here he meets the product at first hand.

against Jardine, then Hammond shares in that criticism in proportion to his seniority in the side. And besides the players, there
were the two managers in Warner and R. C. N. Palairet. Warner was
no match for Jardine, reputedly pleading with him to reduce his
leg-side field, and he came back to England saddened by the whole
affair.

The tale of the third Test at Adelaide, 'the most unpleasant
ever played', has often been told: the confrontation between the
co-manager, Warner, and the Australian captain; the insults and
abuse hurled at Jardine and his team. England won by 338 runs,
Hammond making 85 in the second innings played to the tune of a
noisy and insulting crowd. Yet that was when the temper of the
spectators was comparatively mild. An Australian correspondent
remarked that Hammond's dismissal, bowled by Bradman, was
one of the few moments of light relief in the match. Later, Woodfull
was hit by a fast ball outside the off stump. This angered the
crowd and Hammond himself murmured a word of sympathy to
Larwood. Then Larwood set a leg trap and promptly knocked
Woodfull's bat out of his hand. Hammond has described what
happened next: 'Police came pouring in and massed beside the
pavilion ready to deal with a riot if the crowd invaded the pitch.
It was fortunate indeed that the spectators, ranging against the
boundary fence, hooting and roaring with rage, remained where
they were. If one man had crossed that fence, I do not think the
police could have done very much.'

In the calmer pastures of Toowoomba, Hammond made a century against a Queensland Country XII. The MCC in the 'tropical'
part of their tour added the full Queensland State to the list of first-
class sides they had beaten by an innings. The Brisbane Test, for
ever memorable for E. Paynter's 83 with tonsillitis, was won by six
wickets and the Ashes secured. Hammond was pleased that the
Australians came into the English dressing room afterwards for a
drink.

Finally, the Sydney Test gave England a 4–1 success. Hammond
found himself in partnership with the evil genius of the tour,
Larwood. He got his century but the crowd gave their plaudits to
Larwood whose outstanding innings earned him 98, a massive
reception and a howl of disappointment when he was caught. As a
bowler, he would take but one more wicket in his Test career. His
own runs and the fluency with which Bradman at last handled his
bowling took some of the bitterness out of the series. Hammond

ended the most publicised tour in cricket history with an innings of 75, forcing *Wisden*, in pursuit of sufficient superlatives, into the inelegant judgement that it was 'very brilliant'.

The brilliance was translated across the Tasman Sea to New Zealand. His double-century in the first Test was the prelude to an even greater performance in the second. No-one else made many in the England side but he amassed 336 not out. Bradman's 334 was eclipsed. It was, until Sir Leonard Hutton's 364 in 1938, the highest score in a Test match. There were 192 runs in boundaries in an innings of immaculate footwork. He had finally achieved what the Don had achieved several times: a triple-century. The rivalry was always there under the surface, although the business of accumulation meant less to Hammond than to Bradman. Previously, Hammond noted, he had only made a triple-century against schoolboys.

If in Australia, Hammond was not quite the dominating player of four years previously, he had no need to be. The tour had been a technical success on the field. The administrators and diplomats were left to sort out the politics. As for the players, the Australian Test player, J. H. Fingleton, who was then and for the rest of his life a journalist, was later to remark: 'I do not think there was one single Australian batsman who played in those bodyline games who ever afterwards recaptured his love of cricket.'

It had been a tour on the grand scale. Sailing eastwards via the Mediterranean and the Indian Ocean in September, they had returned via the Pacific and Atlantic Oceans. At Honolulu, Hammond had added surfboard riding to his athletic accomplishments. As they entered Vancouver Harbour hundreds of gulls welcomed them. One gull in particular caught every crumb thrown to it – 'the Wally Hammond of gulls,' exclaimed Pelham Warner. So from the beauty of New Zealand, in which Hammond delighted, they came eventually to the panorama of the Canadian Rockies whose crossing he found 'an enthralling experience'. Like Drake, he had circumnavigated the globe. For both, the West Country was the haven to which they returned. Drake might bowl on Plymouth Hoe. Hammond settled for the nets at Bristol.

5

A Reputation Sustained, 1933–34

'Catches in the slips that deserve to be
preserved in the British Museum'.
The *Sunday Dispatch*, 1934

Hammond's contribution to Gloucestershire cricket in 1933 led
H. E. Roslyn, in his report on the county in *Wisden*, to devote a
quarter of his space to that one player:

> Few, if any, cricketers of recent years have, during such a short period
> before the public, done so much as Hammond, not only for the county
> of his adoption, but for England in Test Matches. His grace of style,
> variety of stroke play and, when he is in his best form, his outstanding
> personality, has caused him to be a great attraction wherever he
> appears. As a fieldsman he is an object-lesson to everybody, in his
> favourite position at slip, by his wonderful sense of anticipation and
> accuracy, while it is perfectly certain that had he not been a great
> batsman he would have achieved considerable fame as a bowler.

Free from any responsibilities as vice-captain, he made over
2500 runs for them, including four double-centuries and a century
in each innings at Worcester. He frequently opened the bowling
and there was a week in July at Bristol when his all-round cricket
dominated play every day against Surrey and Nottinghamshire.
After sharing in a double-century partnership with Sinfield and
making 120, he took six Surrey wickets for 26 in 14 overs to help
in their dismissal for 44, their lowest score since the 1890s.
The Nottinghamshire match produced almost a carbon-copy

performance – 140 runs and then 4 for 19 in 14 overs. In the two games he took eight catches out of the 34 wickets which fell. It was a summer in which he secured 50 catches altogether.

Of many glittering performances, perhaps the double-century against Derbyshire was the most outstanding. The runs came in four hours and included 28 boundaries. T. B. Mitchell, the principal Derbyshire bowler at the receiving end of Hammond's onslaught, wrote to me with a wry remembrance of the occasion but with unstinted praise for a batsman who often singled him out for attention – and who had been one of his closer companions on the 1932–33 Australian tour. The records of Hammond's deeds dominated the press and no newspaper acclaimed him more than the *Daily Express* who ranked him 'among the few super-fieldsmen of the game'.

Yet Hammond in his own writing about that year displays a modesty in keeping with his character and a generosity towards fellow-players by expressing in print what he did not find easy to say. He was full of praise for Barnett's batting and Sinfield's bowling, yet both men, in talking to me, could not recall him ever saying as much to them. But, they were quick to add, he did not want to talk about his own performances either. His reticence calls for further comment. Once, an amateur in the Gloucestershire side took a magnificent catch in the slips, fielding next to Hammond. The other players, even in those days of more restrained behaviour on the field, gathered round to offer their praise. But not a word came from Hammond. There could be no question of jealousy. His own status as a catcher was assured a thousand-fold. Much more likely was his failure to realise that what for him was all in the day's work was a spectacular achievement to someone else. I discussed this question of achievement with a fellow cricket writer when watching a Cup Final at Lord's in the 1980s. 'There are 22 players out there,' remarked my colleague. '20 are striving; two have genius.' Presently a catch of breathtaking quality was taken and the point was made. The genius had held what he could expect to hold. He did not even need to look modest about it. Thus Hammond found it difficult to appreciate that a natural achievement for himself represented endeavour and success for others. To this may be added the view that players were merely doing what they were paid to do. Yet if there was a failure to acknowledge achievement, it was not accompanied by a readiness to criticise failure. Colleagues never had to fear his tongue or even the look on his face. You might, many agreed, even earn a 'Bad luck.' It was as if success put you in his class (for the moment, anyway) and therefore worthy of unspoken acceptance. Failure made you mortal, and worthy of forgiveness.

Hammond's attitude did not win him close friends among the players. He was not one to mix with fellow-players after the day's play, preferring to read a book in his hotel bedroom or visit friends. He continued to remain somewhat detached from his colleagues, and success widened the gulf. He became, said one Gloucestershire professional, 'rather an isolated genius so far as the ordinary cricketer was concerned'. His friendships were to be found outside the professional county dressing room. Next door were the amateurs and with the captain in particular, Beverley Lyon, he came to be on good terms. Lyon, his senior by one year, had been educated at Rugby and Oxford. His social background gave him the ease of manner which the younger man sought to emulate. Beverley Lyon and his wife became visitors to the home which Dorothy had made for herself and her husband at their bungalow at Sixty Acres. One neighbour could remember merry parties at the house. Hammond's pursuit of friendships in a social and economic milieu above his own contributes to an understanding of why he made so little effort at friendship with his fellow-professionals. Other guests were often fellow Test cricketers – sometimes Englishmen playing against Gloucestershire, sometimes Australians on tour. Leslie Ames was one who was asked to stay there from time to time. Someone else felt that 'the Hammonds were reasonably well-off by the standards of the 1930s.' Another visitor thought that 'Wally, in his own house, did most of the talking.'

Many sensed that Dorothy had little real interest in cricket but believed that she gave her husband a good home-base to which he could retreat from his life as a sporting celebrity. Many a wife in those days was content to play second fiddle to her husband's career and interests, to run the home and to seek for little beyond it. In this, Dorothy Hammond was similar to countless others. As the wife of a top-class professional cricketer, she had to face the prospect of frequent absences in the summer and of being left alone for long winters. It was an adjustment she found difficult. She was unusual in never seeing her husband off on his winter tours, although she may be given credit for a genuine sadness at his departures which made her reluctant to go to the station.

Another wife who bade farewell to a husband on three occasions for a six-month trip to Australia commented, 'I was pleased my husband was doing so well. I made my own interests.' Dorothy accepted that situation with less equanimity. Some tension in the marriage there was, but it did not show itself in public and no visitor felt ill at ease.

Their home was convenient for Long Ashton golf course. Hammond was a very talented golfer and the game opened up a range of friendships for him with men who might be cricket followers but were not involved in the game on a day-to-day basis. Among such friends was Jack Britton, who had read 'Greats' at Oxford and won an Athletics Blue. He was a golfer, a club cricketer and an organist – in later years he both built one in his own house and presented one to Trinity, his old Oxford college. He was also a highly successful Bristol businessman and he introduced Hammond to men who were to prove useful to him as he began to consider where his future might lie.

In intellectual and cultural terms, Hammond could be no match for Britton. In sporting terms, the two men had something in common. As golfers, they won the Knowle Club Napier Cup four-ball competition. In commercial terms, Hammond learnt much. Jack Britton and his wife made the Hammonds welcome guests at their home at Lodgeside in Kingswood. He remembered Hammond as 'very much a personal friend over many years, a man with extremely good manners in small company but one who was basically very shy'. Part of the appeal of the Britton home was that Hammond could dine there and not be expected to talk cricket. Among professional cricketers of the 1930s, he was somewhat unusual in moving in business circles in his private life.

The first steps towards a business career for himself were taken when he joined the Cater Motor Company, a subsidiary of Henlys Ltd, at Crofton House, Cheltenham Road, Bristol. 'His "name" brought people along to the showrooms to look,' recalled Irene Allison, then a young secretary. 'He was always very friendly to us in the office, never minded signing lots of autographs and one day brought Don Bradman along and introduced us all.' How much work he did is another matter: Leslie Ames remembered going along and seeing his desk-top totally empty! But his prestige was worth a great deal to the Bristol firm and he stayed with them in a sales capacity for several years. His genuine interest in cars was a help. He was variously seen in a Hudson coupé, a Rover or a

Jaguar. The car business was to be a part of his life for the next 30 years.

We must pick up, if briefly, the bodyline debate since it again became an issue in June 1933 and in some degree involved Hammond. The visiting tourists were the West Indians who, in a fine summer, failed as a side to live up to expectations. They lent heavily on the batting of George Headley and the bowling of E. A. Martindale, the one scoring more than twice as many runs as any other player and the other taking far and away the most wickets. Not until the end of May was Constantine available since he was bound by his contract with the Lancashire League club, Nelson. In his first appearance, against a strong MCC side at Lord's, he took four important wickets, including that of Jardine, the England captain. The press made accusations of bodyline bowling, although Constantine's field had fewer men in the leg trap than Larwood had employed. Despite witnessing such bowling at head-quarters itself instead of garnering information at 12,000 miles range, the authorities at Lord's sent a cable to Australia on 12 June – three weeks after the MCC match – describing the short bumping ball delivered to a packed leg-side field as 'leg-theory' and legitimate. Their attitude bade fair to put the 1934 visit of the Australians in jeopardy.

In the meantime, events at home caused some change of attitude. The West Indies went into the second Test at Old Trafford having taken a decision on the train from Stoke-on-Trent (where they had played against Staffordshire and the great Sydney Barnes) to Manchester to employ bodyline bowling. Constantine wrote, 'It would be pleasant to give Jardine and his men a little taste of what they had been handing out in Australia.'

The West Indians made 375, their highest score against England in England, and at one point were 226 for 1. England at once faced Constantine and Martindale, who bowled more than 50 overs between them, a large number of which were 'fast leg-theory with a packed leg-side field,' as *Wisden* put it. Hammond had his chin cut open, retired for a spell and returned to be caught shortly afterwards. Fingleton, who was in England as a reporter, remarked, 'With three stitches in a gaping cut, he looked a very sick warrior.' Jardine displayed great courage and fearlessness in making a century but the Lancashire crowd drifted away from a spectacle which both they and the press rejected. Warner, co-manager of the 1932–33 tour, wrote to the *Daily Telegraph*, as one who thought of himself as a West Indian, to say that he 'had hoped my countrymen would avoid a type of bowling which I believe to be against the best interests in cricket.' Hammond and Constantine discussed what had happened and the two men shook hands to symbolise their rejection of such an unsportsmanlike approach to cricket. Constantine never bowled bodyline again.

A few days later, Hammond dined with his friend Jack Britton at his home. Others were present and he was asked to give his honest opinion of the bodyline bowling he had seen in Australia. He was among friends. There was no need for histrionics and it was not in the nature of the man. He said quietly, 'I found it loathsome and distasteful. It was sheer intimidation. I was ashamed to be a part of it.'

By now the British public were firmly against bodyline bowling and the editor of *Wisden*, Sydney Southerton, who had been in Australia and reported the tour, summed up the matter when he described the performance of Constantine and Martindale as 'a somewhat pale – but no less disturbing – imitation of Larwood in Australia [but] sufficient to convince many people with open minds on the subject that it was a noxious form of attack not to be encouraged in any way.'

To the West Indians' credit, it was not employed in the final Test, which they lost by an innings. Hammond's own contribution to the three Tests was modest in the extreme – 74 runs in all – but he ensured that the West Indians did not forget him entirely by scoring 264 against them for Gloucestershire, contributing to Gloucestershire's highest total at Bristol since 1900.

Of Hammond's contribution to the 1934 Test series against Australia we can be unusually dismissive. He lay tenth in the averages with only Kenneth Farnes, a bowler fast and simple, below him. Not even a half-century graced his record. Perhaps his greatest contribution was to dismiss Ponsford, S. J. McCabe and Bradman in the third Test. Australia regained the Ashes in the Oval Test, an event less important than the spirit in which the games were played. Hammond wrote, 'If there was one thing that most cricketers at that time wanted to do, it was to bury bodyline and forget about it.' This the players on both sides succeeded in doing at the price of dispensing with Jardine's captaincy and the bowling of Voce and Larwood. Hammond acknowledged that the responsibility for holding up the English batting rested largely on himself. Without seeking excuses – since Bradman with an average of 94 in the Tests had also been unwell and subsequently had an emergency appendicitis operation – he privately admitted to having lumbago (which would eventually end his career) and to a persistent sore throat. Publicly, he presented a sphinx-like image, nothing in his manner revealing disappointment or dismay.

The press stood by him. In the Lord's Test he 'bowled magnificently and took catches in the slips that deserve to be preserved in the British Museum,' said the *Sunday Dispatch*. As a slip, he shone 'as a star of the first magnitude,' said the *Daily Telegraph*. The *Daily Mail*, shyly airing the view that he might possibly be omitted, concluded that he was 'worth a place for his fielding and bowling alone!' An instance of his fielding was recalled for me by a spectator at Old Trafford in the third Test.

Woodfull and Oldfield were batting. I happened to look at Hammond who was fielding in the gully and noticed that he looked half asleep and as if he was quite uninterested in the proceedings and I made a remark to this effect to my friend sitting next to me. Verity then bowled the next ball and it was chopped smartly by Oldfield just wide of Hammond's right hand. This apparently half-asleep fielder instantly came to life and as the batsman went for a single, he spun round in a flash and raced after the ball, caught up with it, picked it up with his right hand and still running away from the wicket and without even appearing to look back and with an uncanny sense of direction, flung the ball back under his left arm straight into the hands of the wicket-keeper just above the bails and there was a run out. Every spectator sitting down leapt to his feet, hats were flung into the air and a roar went up unlike anything I have ever heard on a cricket ground. This quite sudden flash of miraculous fielding produced this spontaneous reaction from every spectator who instantly recognised that returning the ball to the wicket-keeper as fast as he did while still running away from the wicket and aiming it with a sense of direction only was in itself superhuman.

He appeared in fewer than half Gloucestershire's matches owing to injury and Test commitments, but those county games provide a totally different picture. As in 1933, there were four scores over 200 for the county. In 20 innings he scored a hundred in eight of them. His 265 not out against Worcestershire at Dudley led one spectator to say that he would never watch a game again: everything else would be an anti-climax. According to my informant, he never did! A very large proportion of the runs was made at Bristol so that it became more than ever a matter of course that the county ground filled when word spread through the city that he was in.

On no occasion were the public more rewarded than one August day when he amassed 302 not out in a Gloucestershire total of over 600. Barnett made 123 in an innings even more spectacular than Hammond's. The contribution of Barnett to Gloucestershire's batting in these years was no less significant for its taking second place to Hammond's. The county depended on its regular professionals such as Barnett, Goddard, Sinfield and Parker (who retired in 1935), all of whom were England players but none of whom was absent from the county side nearly as often as Hammond.

All these runs on the home front were good business for a man to whom the Gloucestershire committee had awarded a benefit 'for his brilliant all-round contribution'. In the last county match before his benefit game he made 265 not out against Worcestershire at Dudley. The match had its curiosities in that Dacre, Barnett and Hammond all made hundreds exactly as they had done in the same game a year earlier. An elderly spectator was moved to write to the local press:

> Sir – I had the pleasure of seeing this great batsman at his best. I have seen most of the great artists – Graces, Fosters, Fry, Ranji, Hayward, Shrewsbury, Gunn, Trumper, Bradman, Murdoch, Jessop, etc – but never seen an innings like this.
>
> What an artist! A dancing master on his feet, quick as a swallow, lissom as a willow; exploiting every stroke – the glide to leg, the square hit to leg, the chop through the slips, the perfect square cut, the forcing forward shot through the covers, the drive to long-off, and that mighty hit to long-on.
>
> I think that one hit to long-on, right out of the ground and over the wall, was the most sensational hit I have ever seen.
>
> A lovely day, a very nice ground, splendid light, wicket not too easy (some got up a bit), a decent crowd, and what a treat they had! They saw Hammond the Great.

So here was some attempt at comparison with the great of the turn of the century and Hammond placed by this observer ahead of them all. The press, without turning to antiquity, felt the same. There is a monotony in the repetitiveness of the headlines in that benefit summer of 1934 – 'Agile Hammond'; 'Brilliant Form of Hammond'; 'Hammond Supreme'; 'Hammond Dazzles'; 'Power of Hammond'. Those hard-pressed sub-editors who offered something else tried 'Happy Hammond'; 'Hammond, Great, Grand and Glorious'; 'Hurricane Hammond'.

In this atmosphere of adulation, Hammond opened the bowling in his benefit match against Hampshire at Bristol on the Saturday of the August Bank Holiday weekend. He had been, he said, 'a prey to acute uneasiness' in case it rained. Rain did not entirely keep away but an interesting match ended in a draw. He made 78 in one innings. Round the ground they had sold a brochure for a shilling dedicated 'to the greatest all-round cricketer of the present generation'.

Hammond himself was touched by the generosity of the cricketing public who contributed over £2500 and whose messages of congratulation poured in from all over the world. This often taciturn man found himself besieged in the streets by those who sought to shake his hand. Plenty of correspondents have testified to the graciousness of his response.

He had not found it easy to say 'thank-you' to the public. As even the text in the souvenir brochure conceded, he was reserved in character and shunned publicity. To say 'thank-you' is the expected thing to do. Those who have never been shy may wonder why an effort is called for. Hammond made that effort.

Shy he may have been but arrogant he was not. A correspondent told me of a Bristol lad, 'a very poor boy', who waylaid him in the street and asked to be shown how to bat. Hammond got out a bat and ball from his bag, gave the lad and his friends a lesson, took his address and came back a day or two later with some old kit for them.

Flanking one side of the county ground at Bristol is a large, gaunt institutional building which was built in Victorian times by a Prussian called George Muller as a philanthropic venture for orphaned children. Muller's Orphanage was home to some 7000 children before closing to become part of Bristol Polytechnic. Watching Gloucestershire cricket was a great delight to many of them. Earlier generations watched W. G. Grace. The final ones saw Hammond. 'We had porridge for breakfast every day. We saved a bit of it to use as paste to stick cuttings of Hammond's performances into old exercise books,' remembers Owen Jones. Hammond brought colour into many a young life and an occasional visit from him there had the hallmark of a royal occasion.

Meanwhile he had continued to meet his obligations as an old boy of Cirencester Grammar School. He returned from time to time to play in the Old Boys' match and, in his benefit year, was also president of the Old Pupils' Association. The *Wiltshire and Gloucestershire Standard* takes up the account of the day's proceedings in 1934:

> The Cirencester Old Grammarians entertained the teams to lunch, at which Mrs Hammond and other ladies were present, Mr Hammond occupying the chair in his capacity of president of the Old Grammarians for the year.
>
> After lunch Mr T. Frazer, the headmaster, said the School was indeed honoured in having with them Mr Hammond, perhaps the most famous cricketer in the world, and also Mr Neale, a really good cricketer and a splendid fellow in the Gloucestershire side.
>
> A large company turned up to witness the match. The School batted first and had scored 50 for five wickets by the lunch interval. After lunch they carried their total to 107.
>
> Hammond and Neale opened the batting for the Old Boys and there was general disappointment when Hammond was caught and bowled by Mr Flexen in the first over. Few would have held the 'stinger' that Hammond returned to the bowler. Neale, however, batted carefully, and with support from Tyrrell and Tranter the School total was passed with the loss of only five wickets.
>
> A second innings followed, the School being dismissed for 70, and when the Old Boys went in again the spectators were given a great treat, for Hammond showed himself in his true form, and, running to meet the ball, he hit freely, his innings of 63, which included a number of sixes, being compiled from four overs in 19 minutes.

This was, of course, a strictly amateur occasion and the only emolument which came the way of the Hammonds was a bouquet to Dorothy. A more professional occasion took place nearby a few weeks later when a Cirencester and District XI played the full Gloucestershire side at Colesbourne Park for Hammond's benefit. The county had been playing Sussex at Bristol and not until a quarter to seven on a mid-August evening did they take the field. But between then and darkness at ten minutes past nine Gloucestershire amassed 250 and the local XI 184. The *Standard* reporter was again on the scene: 'It was cricket with a laugh in almost every stroke.'

The match attracted a huge crowd, special buses being run from Cheltenham and Gloucester. Collectors went round with mugs to collect donations and over £30 was raised. The *Cheltenham Chronicle* carried a double-spread of illustrations of the match with souvenir copies on sale.

A few days later Hammond was at Dumbleton Hall Park leading a Gloucestershire XI against Wyatt's 'All-England XI'. Then he made a journey in late September to Plymouth to play against a Devon and Cornwall XI, and scored some runs with the aid of a runner. Of course these were benefit games and his appearance was expected but by late September, when he felt 'dragged down and unwell', the temptation to have let such games slip by must have been great.

He was, however, not a man to dodge his cricketing obligations. At the height of his fame, he was much in demand to appear at fund-raising occasions quite apart from his own benefit. One Bristol club, St George's, had secured his services for an evening game whose proceeds would go towards a new pavilion. Many hundred tickets had been sold in the expectation of his appearance. At five o'clock on the day concerned, the organisers received a message from the county ground to say that Hammond had played a long innings and had immediately gone out to field. He would be on the field until half past six and there could be no question of his attendance. Another county player was suggested as an alternative.

The organisers, dismayed, sent a representative to the ground to meet Hammond as he came off the field to try persuasion. There was no need. He had not even known of the telephone call to 'protect' him and at once got into a waiting car without question. He was still in his cricket clothes and he had indeed been on the field virtually all day. But he went straight out to bat at seven o'clock for the Invitation XI, scored a century, fielded, signed autographs, made conversation to his hosts and asked to be driven back to his own car at ten o'clock. The incident, small in itself, was much to his credit.

Hammond, as the 1934 season ended, was still only 31. In the seven years since he had entered Test cricket and the 14 since he had first played for Gloucestershire, he had established a claim to be the finest all-rounder in the world. He was a man with a presence, striking in looks though not of great height. His thick crop of dark hair parted almost in the middle was carefully brushed and his face was still young, fresh and unlined. His reputation as a well-dressed man was established. His benefit of nearly £3000 had given him what many a professional man took six years to earn.

Yet those who knew him closest detected a note of sadness.

They suspected that his marriage had not proved entirely happy. The cricket wives met Dorothy, for in those days Gloucestershire professionals' wives often helped to do the teas for the players. They sensed her resentment at his necessary absences through the game's demands. She had never come to terms with those absences not only abroad but for the day-to-day business of county cricket. Car and train journeys in those pre-motorway days were tedious and long. In the 1980s a player could leave home very early from Bristol and be in time for a match at Leeds or Derby or Manchester. In the 1930s many hours of travelling, and far more nights away from home, were involved. Sunday, though free, might be spent in some distant county town. Dorothy, in the view of someone who knew her very well, was not someone to adapt or to make the best of circumstances.

The absence of children also weakened the marriage. Hammond was devoted to children, as many people have observed, and his delight in other people's children was apparent. He was to admit in later years to a few confidants that their absence was the great tragedy of his marriage. Dorothy also had her confidantes. To them, she conveyed the message that she was not prepared to bring up children alone with an absentee husband.

The marriage had also been put under some strain by the death of Dorothy's father, Joe Lister. After his death his business collapsed under the Depression as the price of wool dropped. Dorothy ceased to have a private income. The economic circumstances of the Hammond household became relatively less prosperous. This is to take purely a mercenary view, but an important one in the context of Hammond's approach to money. Yet it must be said that Joe Lister had been a good friend to his son-in-law, who missed his company. The Lister home in the North was one of the many houses to which he would go during a nearby cricket match. A part of him, as we have seen, was always looking for the family life which had ended so abruptly for him in 1918. One close friend of his mother believed that it was the warmth of the Lister household's welcome rather than the attraction of Dorothy Lister which led him to marry into the family. Hammond was, in 1934, a household name. His own household gods had dealt less kindly with him.

6

The Professional Bows Out, 1934–37

'He is cricket itself'.
The Times, 1937

The s.s. *Cavina*, bound for the West Indies with a cargo of cricketers and anxious to exchange it for a hold of Jamaican bananas, entertained her passengers to a Christmas dinner of turkey and plum pudding two days out from Barbados. After the meal there was deck cricket between the Cavorters and the Rollers, and a swim in the pool.

Hammond was making his second trip to the West Indies, not really fit and hoping that a sea voyage and some months of sunshine would restore him to full health. The side was led by Wyatt, who was supported in batting by Hammond himself, Ames, Maurice Leyland and Hendren, with Farnes, Jim Smith and Eric Hollies as the main attack. The tour began with two matches against Barbados at Kensington Oval. The *Barbados Advocate* set the scene at this 'historic venue of many a dour struggle between the giant kings of the willow of a former day. Four thousand spectators looked on at the players, immaculately dressed in their silks and flannels, dotted here and there over the chlorophyll-coloured carpet of the outfield.'

Here, in the second match, Hammond made 281 not out, sharing in a remarkable last-wicket stand of 122 with Smith. With over 240 to his credit, he was content to let Smith get most of the runs with towering sixes putting at risk those spectators hanging on to the branches of palm trees.

The first Test produced scarcely more runs in all than Hammond himself had made a few days earlier. On the rain-affected wicket England declared at 81 for 7, 21 behind the West Indians. They in turn declared, leaving England 73 to win which, with a struggle, they got. Hammond was top scorer in both England's innings, winning the match with a six over the long-off boundary. He described that pitch as the worst he ever met and his own task as one of the hardest ever required of him. As an assessment of his own abilities, the comment is revealing, the more so as he had nothing to say about his earlier massive score of nearly 300.

From the freshness of Barbados to the humidity of Trinidad was a night's voyage. Port of Spain was then the only centre of first-class cricket in the island and the Trinidad XI was as cosmopolitan as the colony's population with the two Chinese, Tang Choon and Achong, playing besides those of Negro, Indian and White Creole extraction. Learie Constantine, barred from inter-colonial cricket because he was a professional, made his first appearance for Trinidad for four years but the show was stolen by a young unknown called Maynard who made a double-century but achieved little cricketing fame thereafter. Hammond's contribution to a drawn but exciting game was a century.

In the second Test which followed, he made the slenderest of impacts. The match itself was memorable for a great West Indian victory before 11,000 spectators. With two balls remaining Constantine, whose match it was in every sense, trapped Leyland lbw. This was only the second Test match ever to take place in Trinidad. The cricket public would have to wait 14 years for another. Hammond was caught up in the infectious excitement of these West Indians and wrote, 'Every tree instantly deposited all it had. The crowd rushed the pitch and chaired the winners off to the accompaniment of such shouting as I have seldom heard!'

Among the spectators was a 13-year-old boy who would be in the West Indies Test side himself five years later. Jeffrey Stollmeyer's 'first impression was one of awe and majesty and it was an impression which persisted with the passage of time.'

As if it were a statutory command from each colony in turn, Hammond duly made a century against British Guiana, no mean achievement on two counts: the conditions on a rain-damaged wicket had caused 15 wickets to fall for 98 runs before he batted, and his night's sleep had been at a premium in rooms only half-partitioned because of heat where snores, the croaking of frogs,

the ambitions of mosquitoes and Wyatt's early-morning gramo-
phone competed for the sufferer's attention.

The century itself, the British Guiana authorities thought, was
Hammond's hundredth and produced champagne, but the sums
were wrong. *The Times* in England reported that he had made his
ninety-ninth and that English spectators would be unlikely to see
him make his hundredth with the Jamaican part of the tour to
come. But Hammond failed to oblige the Jamaican crowds and he
ended the tour modestly. He topped the batting averages for the
first-class matches but he had failed to make a half-century in the
Tests. By his own standards he had faltered but he had enjoyed his
second – and last – visit to the Caribbean. He felt better and he
wondered why people chose to live in an English climate when
there were such 'paradises on earth as the West Indies'. Homeward bound, this time sharing the passage with bananas, it was
pleasanter to remember Jamaica's Blue Mountains and Barbados
beaches than the steaming heat of Trinidad and the jungles of
Guiana.

To Hammond, the summer of 1935 was 'one of the most
miserable and unlucky seasons of my life'. The ill-health of the year
before returned, he developed septic tonsillitis, found eating
difficult, 'breathing an agony and sleep impossible'. But the total
professionalism in him accepted the requirement to play.

His problems were aggravated by appallingly cold weather
culminating in a snowstorm in the Yorkshire match, and by the
eagerness of the press to record his hundredth hundred. As
with Jack Hobbs a few years earlier, that final century seemed
tantalisingly hard to get. 'Hammond fails again' was not just a sub-
editor's caption for an 80 or 90 somewhere. It served for scores
which on seven occasions were under 20. The undergraduates
flocked to the Parks when the news went round Oxford on two
successive days that he was in the sixties.

The century came against Somerset at Bristol on 13 June. The
final 19 runs took over an hour before he achieved a feat which
had taken only 12 years and of which he was the ninth performer.
The press gave him a great deal of coverage and awaited events in
the first Test against South Africa two days later. 'How we longed
to see Hammond get runs. He looked splendidly confident,' reported the *Daily Telegraph*, but his score of 28 was scarcely
enough. The same paper, a few days later, called for 'a Hammond
century of the true vintage'. Again, his scores were slight and the

press began to debate the case for Hammond staying in the England side. The statisticians accorded him a batting average of 23.47 for the preceding 14 Tests. On the whole, the judgement was that class must prevail: 'a man we cannot leave out'; 'the only one in the side who looked like a real cricketer at Lord's'; 'at any moment he might be worth 200 runs'. When he was selected for the third Test, with 160 at Worcester to back the case, the critics welcomed the choice. If he comes off, said the *Daily Telegraph*, 'onlookers will witness batting that no other cricketer on earth can better.' If he doesn't come off, said the *News Chronicle*, 'we may be in the position of having to play in the subsequent Tests without one of the three greatest all-round cricketers in the world.'

That third Test at Leeds saw Hammond return to form with 63 and 87 not out. Those Tests were only allocated three days and runs had to be got quickly against a side which Hammond himself rated 'the strongest that had ever come out of South Africa', though the absence of Xenophon Balaskas through injury weakened the bowling.

The papers were full of pictures of Hammond batting. He was 'the Hammond of legend, the scourge of bowlers all the world over. He made every other batsman in the match look second-rate by comparison and he was the pattern of a great cricketer.' He twice dismissed Bruce Mitchell, South Africa's dour and experienced opening batsman, and took three catches, one of which was deemed 'a catch in a million' to dismiss I. J. Siedle. *Wisden* called it a 'memorable incident of the match' and photographs reveal the effortless and graceful way in which Hammond could swoop down and take the ball inches from the ground. Only Hammond himself was downcast. The tonsillitis dragged on and he felt ill. Yet he managed to top the England batting averages for the series and the national averages for the season.

The Cricketer had an extended correspondence on his standing in the gallery of great all-rounders. He was being set against George Hirst and Rhodes, to his disadvantage, but the view was widely expressed that his greatest days had yet to come. During the correspondence, P. F. Warner, editor of *The Cricketer* and always one of Hammond's greatest supporters, drew readers' attention to his performance against Leicestershire in which he made 252, took 4 for 41 and made five catches.

Hammond had been in the game 14 years or so and a long future was predicted for him. The *Daily Mail* saw him easily eclipsing

Hobbs' 197 centuries and being in the game until 1955. Few, and certainly not Hammond himself, would have guessed that he had only five full English seasons remaining. He himself, through a combination of reasons, was in something of a mid-career crisis, depressed and despondent with himself and making more of a brace of ducks in the Scarborough Festival than of the good things which had come his way that summer.

There had been, for instance, a game at Canterbury before a sweltering August Bank Holiday crowd for W. H. Ashdown's benefit. Hammond and Sinfield put on 187 in two hours. 'Sinfield was the honest workman, but only by comparison, for most batsmen would be nowhere with Hammond, the patrician of batsmen, at the other crease. He drove with a power and nobility that made us gasp,' reported a Kent journalist. A century at Folkestone had given him some personal pleasure. Cricket at Folkestone, he said, was fun, and to be followed with 'the finest Kentish nut-brown ale'.

His status in the game at this stage may be measured by the placing of his name – and the only professional so named – in the distinguished guest-list at the Dorchester Hotel to bid farewell to Jack Hobbs in first-class cricket. Among famous names present were the Earl of Rosebery, Hobbs' county captain at the turn of the century, E. V. Lucas, the essayist and editor of *Punch*, and J. B. Priestley, the novelist.

The 1935 cricket season had seen the introduction of the experimental lbw rule, designated in the scoresheets as lbw(N), whereby a batsman might be out to a ball pitching on the off-side of the striker's wicket which would have hit it if not intercepted by the striker's person between wicket and wicket at the point of impact. The law was designed to reduce high scoring and the number of drawn games. Hammond's figure of 49.35 was the lowest average to top the national list since the wet summer of 1910, so that the amendment, soon made permanent, had its desired effect. Hammond was with the great majority in welcoming the change.

Meanwhile, the first hint that Hammond might cease to be a professional emerged in the Gloucestershire committee minutes for January 1936. The chairman, A. J. Gardner, was instructed to see if he would be prepared to play as an amateur, be appointed assistant secretary and share the captaincy with B. H. Lyon. Gardner and Hammond met but Hammond felt unable to accept the offer on financial grounds. Indeed, he would have been paid less as assistant secretary than his £450 as senior professional. The man eventually appointed instead was paid £200 a year. But Hammond asked for the matter to be left open for another year and, as a gesture to the club at a time of financial strain, waived his claims for 'talent and wins' money for the coming season. In the end the side in 1936 was led by neither Lyon nor by Hammond but by a young amateur, D. A. C. Page, who was killed in a car crash just after the season ended.

The throat infection which had worried Hammond for over a year led to the removal of his tonsils just before the 1936 season began. The operation left him weak. He returned to cricket too soon, performed indifferently and was persuaded to take a genuine rest, thus missing a Test match for only the second time until his final game in Australia ten years later.

The Gloucestershire committee decided after much discussion to give him £25 towards the cost of his hospital expenses. At the same time they agreed to regularise the position of professionals' insurance against accident and sickness and informed Hammond that his award was 'an act of grace which did not establish a precedent'. It was late July before he felt restored to health and he marked that event by a display of batting between then and the end of season which delighted his public, forced the critics to search for fresh hyperboles and re-wrote the records in the next year's *Wisden*.

India were the victims of his onslaught in the second and third Tests. Howard Marshall, pioneer of cricket broadcast commentators, declared that Hammond had 'entered his kingdom again, fit and confident, master of himself and the occasion.' His 167 at Old Trafford found him constantly forcing the ball off his back foot to the boundary and cutting with precision and power. The *News Chronicle* believed the Test match had been staged in his honour. His 217 at the Oval, said the *Daily Mail*, 'dwarfed every other incident. Grey-headed veterans forgot Trumper and MacLaren and sat staring at Hammond's almost insolent display.' L. V. Manning in the *Daily Sketch* withdrew his belief that half-a-crown was too much to charge for admission to a Test if Hammond were batting. When he was out, later spectators should pay only a shilling. That innings at the Oval was used by his teacher to encourage a small boy at a nearby Kennington elementary school to emulate his namesake and pull his socks up. So remembered Ted Hammond, who has gone through life known as 'Wally'. Hammond himself did not underrate the Indians, regarding them as 'very tough and worthy opponents' who would 'one day challenge England on absolutely equal terms'.

Meanwhile, Gloucestershire fortunes needed the help of their principal performer, the more so as Parker had retired after a long and distinguished career. The county rose 11 places in the Championship to finish fourth. The old-established batsmen were joined by Jack Crapp, and Barnett emerged as the season's principal run-getter. Sinfield and Goddard, in his benefit year, captured most of the wickets.

Hammond scored 160 not out on the first day of August against Somerset and made runs of some substance for the county in every remaining match. At the very end of the month he scored 317 against Notts at Gloucester in Goddard's benefit match and, by reaching a total for the month of 1281 runs, he eclipsed the previous record, established by W. G. Grace in 1876. Goddard benefited from a record crowd of 7000 and from the gift by Hammond of his bat for auction, while the *Gloucester Citizen* next morning marked the event with a leading article entitled 'From Grace to Hammond'. The triple-century against Notts, with Larwood and Voce playing, was a counter to those who doubted his abilities against a really fast attack.

Gloucestershire's match against Yorkshire at Sheffield was an occasion recalled by Sir Leonard Hutton. 'I took away the memory of a gigantic and unbroken third-wicket stand by Barnett and Hammond,' he recalled. From that point onwards, Hutton believed in Hammond's greatness and came to see him as the greatest cricketer he had ever played with or against. His greatness was 'an all-round greatness'. It was a remark in line with a Cardus judgement of that summer: 'He is a Jessop one day, a WG another. Perhaps posterity will rank him the greatest of all.'

Hammond's third passage to Australia was of course assured, but an interesting pointer to the future was raised by his captaincy of the Players against the Gentlemen. Charles Bray wrote in the *Daily Herald* that his leadership in that match 'was the talk of the astute critics'. Bray added his own astute judgement that Hammond had 'on previous occasions shown himself to be a fine captain when he has a good side to lead'. Later, events in 1938 and 1946 would support Bray's view. Meanwhile, he regretted that Hammond's professional status forbade his leading the forthcoming side to Australia.

Hammond was more than delighted with the man who was appointed captain. G. O. Allen, who had led England that summer against India, was 'worth a nip of champagne all round to any team, a popular leader whom nothing could shake'. But Hammond would again be the sheet-anchor of a side dispatched not only to win back the Ashes but also to restore goodwill after the 1932–33 tour. In an open letter to Allen, the *Illustrated Sporting News* saw Hammond as the 'commanding player' both in temperament and technique. The press as a whole placed a heavy reliance on Hammond's batting as England's answer to Bradman. The *Daily Herald* sent him on his way with the comment that 'Style is the man.'

Pre-war cricket tours to Australia were long-drawn-out affairs, taking their participants away from England in early September and not bringing them home until late April. Wives, forbidden by contract to accompany their husbands, were left alone or with families to look after for a lengthy English winter. The farewells at St Pancras Station or Tilbury Docks had a poignancy lacking in the cool, impersonal airport lounges of our own day. Hammond's departure overseas was something to which his wife Dorothy never became reconciled but her concern for her husband was undoubted. When a dog-bite laid her low for some weeks she was anxious that no report of it should reach Australia. Only when she was on the road to recovery did she telephone him both to break the news and to congratulate him on opening the tour with four successive centuries. For he had landed at Perth feeling 'wonderfully fit and happy', promptly scored two centuries and added two more (in one game) at Adelaide. Four in a row had brought him into a select group eclipsed only by C. B. Fry's six in 1901. Fry himself was a spectator at that Adelaide game.

By way of a change, Hammond then switched his energies to bowling, taking 5 for 39 against New South Wales. Since his efforts (and 91 runs as well) failed to prevent MCC losing the match, there was something to be said for the *Daily Mail*'s comment that 'he *was* the team.' The *News Chronicle* published a 'Mercer' cartoon in which Hammond was seen to be doing everything in the side – batting, bowling, keeping wicket and umpiring. These interpretations by the English press would not have appealed to Hammond himself and were soon at a discount. His county colleague Barnett made 259 against Queensland looking, Hammond wrote, 'one of the most graceful and assured batsmen England has ever produced'. Then came the first Test. It was won for England by the bowling of Allen and Voce who dismissed Australia for 58 in the second innings in 12.3 overs. 45 years later both men could recall the thrill of that glorious hour made the more possible by a sticky wicket.

So to the second Test at Sydney and to one of the majestic innings of Hammond's career. He batted most of the first day for 147 and throughout the second, limited by rain, to reach 231 not out. The old Australian player, Clem Hill, declared that the innings put him on a par with Bradman as a batsman. That other 'Hill', the Sydney crowd, roared their approval, crying to their own bowlers, 'You'll-never-get-him-out.' R. C. Robertson-Glasgow, the stylish critic of the 1930s, wrote:

> I know of no match in which each batsman has so subordinated his art and inclinations to one master. Ames and Hardstaff, both batsmen of personal ideas, went in to join Hammond, just batted at the other end, and in due time left the presence. Even Henry Irving needed the support of his cast who spoke a line or so then went their unknown ways. But Hammond needed nothing: an extraordinary achievement of will, skill, eye and muscle. Nothing more magnificent has been done in athletics in many years.

A victory by an innings which his batting had nurtured was brought to fruition by his bowling contribution which clinched England's superiority and left her two up in the chase for the Ashes. To those at home, the news was a tonic and an uplift from the depressing news of the Abdication. Australians were not so sure, for Edward VIII was their king too. They had lost both a Test match and a monarch.

With the success achieved so far England had to be content. Not another first-class match on the mainland did they win. Australia won the three remaining Tests and held the Ashes. Too much was asked of Hammond. 'Did England give up hope when Hammond was out?' asked the *Daily Express* of the third Test. He had made 32 runs out of a total of 76 in an innings which he believed was one of the best of his career. On a wicket nasty, difficult and fiery, he alone gave substance to the batting. In the fourth Test at Adelaide England were in with a chance on the final day, following Hammond's 5 for 57 in Australia's second innings, until he was bowled in the first over, an event which the *Sydney Morning Herald* regarded as clinching victory for Australia.

The last Test at Melbourne, with the two sides even, brought Australia's highest innings ever against England in Australia, 604. The Australian device of using Bill O'Reilly to bowl at Hammond's leg stump achieved some measure of success, for O'Reilly dismissed him twice in the match. One paper described the two men as 'the major public attractions in the game'. Without a significant contribution from Hammond, England slipped to defeat by an innings and 200 runs. It would be fair to add that in the series as a whole they had had the worst of the luck in terms of wet wickets.

Hammond topped the tour averages for batting and was third as a bowler. The former Australian opening batsman, Macartney, whom Hammond had so much admired in 1921, summed up his part in the tour:

> England have in Hammond the finest all-round cricketer in the world. No Australian can compare with him in that respect. He possesses a wonderful temperament. He has a philosophical attitude to success or failure which, combined with his immense experience, makes him of great assistance to his captain.

In *The Cricketer* Spring Annual the claim was made that he towered majestically above all others as a batsman on all wickets although the palm was still given to Bradman on true wickets. So ended a tour which Hammond believed was one of the happiest of his life, made up of men 'on the best of terms with one another'.

Homeward bound, MCC sailed eastwards across the Pacific to Honolulu and Hollywood. Their host at the film studios was the old England cricketer, Sir C. Aubrey Smith, who arranged for them to watch the filming of *The Prisoner of Zenda*. A land journey brought them to New York and an Atlantic voyage to Southampton. Almost within hours, Hammond was batting at Southampton 'at his most regal and significant', according to *The Times*, with strokes which would be remembered long after the season was ended. All this was as early as 5 May, with a whole summer to be savoured. Next day, he was picking up Hampshire wickets to the tune of 5 for 30.

In that same game against Hampshire, Barnett, his colleague in Australia, took 5 for 40 and made a century. In the Gloucestershire averages of the season just beginning he would finish second to Hammond, as he had done in the Australian tour averages. Players of Barnett's calibre must from time to time have felt that however well they might play, Hammond could better their performance.

They would have been less than human if they had not felt a pang of envy from time to time. Hammond remained a modest commentator on his own achievements. Pride was banished to the margins of his make-up. Yet this basically shy man laid himself open to the charge of arrogance through his slowness to bestow congratulations on his county colleagues. Was it because he did not want to seem to be patronising them? The plaudits were reserved for the opposition, into whose dressing room he was ready to wander. His own team-mates had to read them in his books published after he had retired. All this goes some way to explaining why it was my experience, in discussing Hammond with so many of his contemporaries, to find that those who knew him as an opponent or as an England colleague spoke more warmly of him than did his county colleagues. The reserve which was so much part of Hammond's make-up made him paradoxically less willing to show his true feelings to those with whom he spent the most time.

Those runs at Southampton were the prelude to one of Hammond's greatest seasons. He scored over 3000 runs for an average of 65.04, including 13 centuries. He took 33 wickets for Gloucestershire and was second to Goddard in the averages, twice bowling unchanged throughout an innings. Of all his appearances in 1937 two stood out above all others. He played for the North against the South in a match commemorating the hundred and fiftieth anniversary of the foundation of MCC. His 86 and 100 not out, said the newly knighted Sir Pelham Warner, was 'an object lesson in the art of playing slow bowling', while his 'placing of the faster bowlers, with oceans of time for the stroke, was supreme,' wrote Howard Marshall. 'He is cricket itself,' said the correspondent of *The Times*, 'and it is right that he should have made the runs in this week of commemoration.' Voce, who caught him superbly, felt almost sad to see him go. Wilfrid Brookes, the editor of *Wisden*, joined in the praise despite being at the receiving end of a six into the press box: 'But what a shot! The power, the superb driving, the grace of it will remain in my memory. Decapitation was a cheap price to pay.'

The other occasion was at Lord's in the first Test against New Zealand. It was, curiously, his first century in a Test on that ground and he made it one to remember for the mastery he acquired over a sound attack backed up by excellent fielding. He and Joe Hardstaff, emerging as a player of great elegance and style, each made centuries while Barnett, again playing second string to Hammond, made 83 not out.

It was a season of personal records for Hammond – more centuries than any other Gloucestershire player when he passed W. G. Grace's 126, most Test appearances for England when he passed Woolley's 64. The *Daily Mail* computed what he would accomplish by the end of his career. The figures prophesied for him were very close to those actually held by Hobbs, who had retired in 1934. He would score 60,664 runs and make 191 centuries. The estimate proved wildly wrong: he was to score 50,551 runs and make 167 centuries. Journalists as well as politicians had their heads in the sand in 1937. Hammond would lose six years of his playing career to the war.

When Hammond walked off the field at the Folkestone Festival one September evening after playing for the Over-Thirties against the Under-Thirties, he walked into the pavilion for the last time as a professional. There was a touch of humour at the end. The Under-Thirties had dropped a few catches. In Hammond's handwriting a note was pinned up in their dressing room: 'Catching for the Babes at 10.00 a.m.'

But at 34 he was at the pinnacle of his career and had left 'The Babes' far behind. He was the most famous person in Bristol. He played golf with the city's businessmen and was welcome at Badminton, the home of the Duke of Beaufort. Well-dressed in double-breasted suits or plus-fours as fitted the occasion, commanding attention wherever he went, he had aspired to a social status no English professional cricketer, not even Jack Hobbs, had approached. But on the £400 or so a year which Gloucestershire paid him, together with his job with Henlys, he found it a struggle to keep up appearances. Dorothy tried unsuccessfully to get a job in a gown shop to supplement their income.

Friends in the business world such as Jack Britton believed that there was no future for him in Cater's and he himself felt the same. There were other and better prospects. Talk and influence contributed to the chain of events which led in November 1937 to Hammond changing his employers and becoming an amateur. The professional had bowed out.

7

England Captain, 1938–39

'A captain to the manner born.'
The *News of the World*, 1937

An astute observer, walking through Marsham Street in West-minster in the spring of 1920, might have spotted a sign strung up on a door by an old bootlace inviting callers to enter. Inside he would have found Charles and Tom Guyatt, two young men trying to set up a business after the first world war. The idea was right, for they aimed to meet the demand for tyres and tubes in the new age of the car and charabanc. London chauffeurs flocked to them to get a rapid tube-repair service. The marketing of tyres prospered and soon there were branches outside London. In 1925 the firm of Marsham Tyres opened in Bristol. In the years between then and 1939 its expansion into the largest business of its kind in Europe marched hand in hand with the cricketing successes of Gloucestershire's Wally Hammond.

Marsham men in Bristol knew Hammond as a salesman with Cater's. They took time off to watch him play cricket and they met him on the golf course. When the whisper grew that he would like to turn amateur, Charles Guyatt, the managing director, invited Hammond to join the board of directors of Marsham Tyres. The initial offer had not been for a directorship, but Hammond's business friends in Bristol urged him to accept nothing less.

The press were invited to the Old Cheshire Cheese in London's Fleet Street to meet the new director on 9 November 1937 when Hammond quipped, 'It's time I did a job of work.' Guyatt commented that he would be able to play as much cricket as he liked in the immediate future. The announcement was linked to the English captaincy and indeed, that prospect was in the minds of his new employers. Approaches had been made by influential members of MCC to Dunlop, the parent company, towards the possibility of Hammond being made financially independent of cricket. With a director's salary of £2000 he had become, by the standards of the time, well-off.

Hammond's value to Marsham Tyres lay in the contacts he was able to make. Bill Pope, a fellow-director and subsequently managing director after the second world war, remembered the contribution he made to the firm:

> Whether on cricket tours or playing in England, on the golf course or at some dinner, he brought us business. He had an easy manner, a memory for names and, of course, great prestige. In the continuing growth years of 1938 and 1939, despite the European political un-certainty, he was involved as our firm's main outside 'contact' man.

Pope admitted that the glamour of bringing in business appealed to Hammond more than the routine of following it up, but his job remained clear – to get the orders. He was popular with the firm's representatives and surviving photographs show him smiling at golfing functions and office gatherings. In attracting to their ranks one of the best-known figures in England, Marsham Tyres had done themselves a service. By 1939, an expansion pro-gramme which some had felt to be too ambitious had proved over-modest. New production facilities could scarcely meet increasing demand.

Then came the second world war. The firm contributed to the wartime needs both for tyres and for man-power. Hammond left them to join up and the job awaited his return. His value to Marsham had been as much on the cricket field as off it. In the 22 months he was with them until war broke out he played two English seasons and undertook one overseas tour. As the press had predicted, he did so as captain of England. Speculation had begun as soon as he turned amateur. In February 1938 a former England captain, R. W. V. Robins, declared at a public function, 'No cricketer would object to being led by such a great player as Wally Hammond.' What seems obvious to a later generation was less so at that time. For a professional to captain a twentieth-century England side was unthinkable; for an ex-professional to do so was only barely tenable. He had been 'one of the finest and most brainy of the Players' captains against the Gentlemen,' said the *News of the World*. 'He was a captain to the manner born.' The *Daily Mail* agreed with the sentiment but believed that 'the strangling effect of the old school tie' would prevent his selection.

A few months after he had turned amateur he was appointed England captain for the Test trial and then for the first Test against Australia. Seven centurions rather than he stole the limelight in a high-scoring game at Trent Bridge. His Gloucestershire colleague, Sinfield, secured Bradman's wicket in what proved to be his only Test. Hammond the captain was launched. Hammond the batsman kept himself for the second Test.

A beguiling calm engulfed the people of Britain in the last week of June 1938. Domestic events dominated the press and the sporting world followed the athletic performances of Sidney Wooderson, the miler, and of Henry Austin at Wimbledon. The *Daily Sketch* was selling sun lotion to its readers for threepence and a young man called Viscount French made a half-century in the Winchester v. Eton match. His grandfather had been the first commander of the BEF in the first world war and it was the memories of that war which the British public still put sternly on one side.

But the voice of Winston Churchill compelled attention. Europe, he declared, was 'confronted with a programme of aggression'. His son-in-law, Duncan Sandys, had that month quoted in Parliament figures which revealed the weakness of British defences. Hitler's incorporation of Austria was a matter of recent history. Czechoslovakia was mentioned in the press, and not just for her entrants at Wimbledon.

Three pictures dominated the tabloid press on Saturday 25 June 1938. One was of the British and Italian fleets in Valetta harbour, Malta, with the caption, 'Peace and strength blend in perfect harmony: the friendliness of two great nations.' The second showed Stanley Baldwin, the former prime minister so often identified with the mood of the nation, who was the current president of MCC, introducing the England captain, W. R. Hammond, to King George VI. The third picture caught the image of a Hammond cover drive in the second Test.

There was something very special about that Test match at Lord's in 1938. MCC had commissioned the Royal Academician, Charles Cundall, to paint the scene in oils. His picture conveys the atmosphere of those days – a Lord's undwarfed by surrounding high buildings except for two blocks of flats; the old Tavern and the soft felt hats and flannel 'bags' of the spectators. Yet something is lacking. Perhaps the artist, in his attempt to portray the tranquillity of Lord's capped by a clear blue sky and some benevolent white clouds, allowed the scene to be too benign. As in the Europe of that June, so at Lord's, a passiveness of mood was matched by activity. No-one would guess from Cundall's picture that Hammond had chosen the moment to play one of the finest innings of his resplendent career. Nor indeed had the artist found a way to record the historic importance of the beginning of Test match television presentation, for it was in this game that the now-familiar cameras and their crews first came to Lord's and H. B. T. Wakelam presented the first commentary.

When Hammond came in to play his second innings as an England captain, 3 wickets were down for 31 runs taken by the Australian fast bowler, E. L. McCormick, in just 25 deliveries. When he was dismissed the total was 457. He had batted for six hours and his 240 was the highest score for an England player in any home Test – though that record would last only until August.

The chairman of the selectors, Sir Pelham Warner, believed no finer innings on a good wicket could be imagined. It was 'Hammond at his best, cool and unruffled and masterly both in defence and stroke play. He was never once beaten by any bowler.' Sir Donald Bradman commented that he could recall 'no instance when Hammond's superb artistry showed so brilliantly'. Denis Compton recalled it as 'vintage Hammond evoking praise from even the most hardened professional'. To Sir Leonard Hutton, it was an occasion 'superb and masterly'. All the survivors of that Test to whom I talked were unanimous in their judgement. Only Fingleton qualified his view by rating the innings of Barnett in the preceding Test as even greater. Barnett himself, so often second string to Hammond, was generous in his tribute.

To the praise of the players we may add that of the critics. *The Times* wrote:

> The first day's play will be remembered by all those who were lucky enough to be there for a display of batting by Hammond which can seldom have been surpassed. He has never approached such grandeur. It was a combination of batting technique and cricket brain supported by physical endurance which was amazing. His century was marked up on the score-card from the moment he came in. It was

an innings superlative in conception and perfect in execution. Mere figures cannot express the virtue of his performance.

Cardus, in the *Manchester Guardian*, commented:

Using all the proportion I can master, I declare that Hammond batted with an ease and style beyond anything he has ever done before: more handsome cricket could not be imagined. He drove almost nonchalantly. The swift velocity of his late cuts seemed an optical illusion. The wrists were supple as a fencer's steel.

The spectators had greeted his arrival at ten minutes past twelve, cheered his century at seven minutes past three, and departed for their trains at eleven minutes past six when he reached his double-century. A record crowd of thirty-three thousand came the next morning and saw Hammond make a further 30 runs.

For those spectators at Lord's in 1938 there was an image to take away and to savour; a moment of happiness to recapture as world events took their course; a distant recollection to be won back from the depths of memory in the post-war years. Cardus, too, had sensed the mood of that Test match. 'The sunshine blessed all, King and people. This was Lord's in June. If Hitler could have looked on the scene, he would have said, "Still kicking a cricket ball around."'

Men, now old in the 1980s, had taken that Friday off work, and their proud boast remains that they 'saw Hammond make that double-century at Lord's.' Men, not yet old, went as boys with their fathers and the day made them the game's slaves for ever. The scene when Hammond was out, wrote Cardus, 'was surely one of the greatest tributes ever paid to a cricketer at Lord's.'

This man had done something for those spectators. What had the occasion done for him? Hammond had walked into the pavilion, Cardus had continued, 'head down and modest'. He himself called it 'the proudest moment of my life'. This was his finest hour. Never again, in the atmosphere of stern, competitive cricket, would he exercise such an unrelenting dominance and display such captivating elegance. With that innings he reached the peak of his career. All else which he would accomplish would, by his own standards, be something less. Of that future he could know nothing with certainty but perhaps there was some sense of awareness. As a cricketer he felt that the years of playing which lay before him were limited and his decision to make his way in business related to this. As a man he had some sense of the course of political events. He was a soldier's son. He has recorded that he felt 'the end of an era was approaching.' For him, as for every cricket supporter, that match at Lord's had its own poignancy.

The game itself was a contest matching the occasion. England's 494 brought an Australian reply of 422 and a double-century by W. A. Brown. An English declaration left Australia little chance of making over 300 and the game was left drawn. Bradman made a century and earlier, Ames and Paynter of the older generation and Compton of the younger had all made runs.

It rained every day at Old Trafford and not a ball was bowled in the third Test. The fourth, at Headingley, brought the Australians victory by five wickets and they kept the Ashes. Hammond and Bradman, the two captains, made the top scores of a low-scoring game. Hammond's 76 was invaluable, especially as England had a side with a particularly long tail. His dismissal first ball in England's second innings, caught in a packed short-leg area, brought total silence from the vast crowd who only seconds earlier had cheered him all the way to the wicket.

The fifth Test at the Oval will always be remembered as 'Hutton's match'. Australia's defeat was more substantial than any side had suffered in the long history of Anglo-Australian games. To England's 903 for 7 declared, Australia replied with 201 and 123. The match was intended to be played to a finish and only the tragedy of injuries to Bradman and Fingleton brought about a merciful declaration from an England side which might have scored 1000. Hutton, in making 364, displayed his patience on the field. Hammond's had to be kept for the dressing room while he watched Hutton and Leyland put on 382 for the second wicket. When eventually he joined Hutton, he stayed to see his own record of a few weeks earlier beaten. He and Hutton shared another substantial partnership of which Hutton remarked, 'To watch him from the other end was to be reminded that cricket is a game of timing and hair's-breadth precision, an object lesson in the craft of playing cricket.'

Hardstaff, who made 169 himself in that Test, remembered Hammond's instruction to him as he went in when the total was 555: 'Play steady!' And he recalled the greatness of Hammond:

> I thought I could play until I batted with him. He made me look like a donkey at the side of a race-course. He was a man with two shots for

any ball, one for his front foot, one for his back. He was without question the finest player in the world, a much greater batsman than Bradman for he could bat on all kinds of wickets.

These four Test matches had been Hammond's apprenticeship as England captain. There was some criticism of his use of bowlers and his county colleague, Sinfield, who played in the second Test, sensed some uncertainty in Hammond's judgement in this area. Hedley Verity bowled only seven overs in Australia's 411 in the first Test and showed in the second what he might have done, conceding only 100 runs in 62 overs. In the fourth Test greater use of D. V. P. Wright (who took 3 for 26 in five overs) could just have stopped an Australian victory. In the fifth Test Hammond was criticised for contemplating a total of over 1000 and declaring only when Australia were down to nine fit men, but the Test was timeless and part of his policy was to prove the nonsense of Tests without a limit.

The overall judgement was that he had led the England side well. The editor of *Wisden* called him 'sagacious and inspiring'. Hammond himself felt he had passed from apprentice to journeyman to master when Lord Hawke, forever remembered as the opponent of a professional captain of England, congratulated him on his performance. He was invited to lead the Gentlemen against the Players at Lord's, becoming and remaining the only man to have captained both sides. The team, which he led to victory, contained one former England captain and two future ones while Hutton, the first professional captain of England, was in the Players' team. The Gentlemen won for only the second time since 1914 and the chairman of the England selectors, Warner, declared that Hammond had led the side splendidly. The occasion clinched his selection as captain of the MCC party which departed for South Africa in the autumn.

Other honours came his way in 1938. Gloucestershire elected both him and his wife to life membership of the Club. He was also elected to membership of MCC. Few men can have had a more distinguished pair to support their nomination: he was proposed by Stanley Baldwin and seconded by the former president of MCC, England captain and Governor of Bengal, Sir Stanley Jackson.

For Gloucestershire, the new life member performed admirably, scoring 15 centuries, averaging over 80, making 500 more than any other player despite frequent Test absences, and scoring two double-centuries. One of them, against Lancashire at Bristol, illustrated his continuing ability to dominate a match if circumstances demanded. Conditions favoured the bowling side and Hammond advised B. O. Allen, the county captain, to put Lancashire in if he won the toss. He did so and Lancashire amassed 426, of which Cyril Washbrook made 219 not out. Gloucestershire, after a strong opening stand, lost wickets regularly. Seven men made under 40 between them. But A. E. Wilson, coming in at no. 9, stayed with Hammond. Their partnership realised 239 and Hammond himself scored 271. Washbrook remembered the occasion. Hammond had remarked to him afterwards that he felt responsible for the decision to put Lancashire in. After the Lancashire innings, he assured Allen that Gloucestershire would score more than Lancashire. At a critical point he protected E. D. R. Eagar (who played for Gloucestershire before becoming captain of Hampshire after the war) from facing a single ball and later nursed Wilson. 'It was a mastery of a situation,' remarked Washbrook, 'of which he was capable up to the war but which was beyond his powers after 1945.' For Washbrook, as for Hardstaff, Hammond was the greatest player he had ever seen. 'He was greater than any other all-rounder.' It was performances such as these that gave Hammond this quality of greatness and which placed him head and shoulders above every contemporary English cricketer.

A strong party sailed under his leadership to South Africa on the *Athlone Castle* in October 1938. Just 12 years earlier, Hammond had come to Cape Town to recuperate at the Green Point Club. In the intervening period he had stamped his indelible mark on the game, and the confidence and assurance which he showed both as captain and player took shape in the South Africa season of 1938–39. The team moved up from the Cape, playing the various provincial sides and carrying all before it until it came to Johannesburg and was lucky to draw with Transvaal. Hammond had made runs in most games and a spectacular century against Natal at Durban. William Pollock, one of only two reporters on the tour from England, wrote ecstatically in the *Daily Express*, 'Hammond gave the spectators the time of their lives as he reduced the bowling to child's play. Time after time he was halfway down the pitch as if having his fun with little boys on Margate sands.' Yet one of those bowlers would later top the South African bowling averages in the Tests!

The most northerly point in South Africa at which they played was Pretoria and the MCC visit coincided with the December celebrations commemorating the centenary of Dingaan's day or the Day of the Covenant. It is an event entrenched in Boer history and marked the victory by the Voortrekers – those who made the Great Trek – over Dingaan, the Zulu chief, in 1838. The symbolism of the Great Trek was re-enacted and Hammond, as England captain, went out early in the morning to greet the incoming ox-drawn wagons treading the original path. Young men dressed up and with beards in the style of their forefathers rode alongside and a great camp was set up for visitors from all over the Union. The Boer War had taken place little more than a generation ago. Some of the cricketers against whom MCC were playing had been born before the Union of South Africa had been established in 1910. Hammond's gesture, and his decision to take the MCC team to a service in Johannesburg Cathedral before playing Transvaal on the actual day of the centenary, was described by one of the side as a 'diplomatic courtesy' in a geographical area of South Africa where memories of the two Anglo-Boer Wars were still strong.

Forty years earlier, another group of English cricketers had been very close to the events which sparked off the second Anglo-Boer War. The visit of Lord Hawke's team to South Africa in 1895–96 coincided with the famous Jameson Raid, an ill-fated attempt by a group of Englishmen to seize the Transvaal and over-throw the Dutch republican government there. The cricketers were quickly sent up from the Cape to Johannesburg to provide a calming influence. Once in Boer territory, they found their train surrounded by Boer farmers with bandoliers and loaded rifles and were required to pay customs duties on all their equipment, even bats. As they entered Johannesburg, there was a major explosion and some loss of life. The Wanderers cricket ground was turned into a hospital and the cricketers were sent 30 miles north to Pretoria. A match was hastily arranged against a Boer XI and played, as C. B. Fry has recorded, 'without any feeling alien to the pleasant rivalry of an English cricket field'. The team even met Paul Kruger, the Boer leader, who gave them coffee. Fry suspected that his reply to Lord Hawke's invitation to watch the match was less polite than that rendered by the interpreter. A few days later a match against a XV of Johannesburg had to be postponed because of the disturbed conditions in the town. But the tour continued. Matches were played in the British areas of the Cape and Natal, and within a few weeks the long train journey north was again being made to play the second Test in Johannesburg. In the view of Field-Marshal Jan Smuts, the Jameson Raid 'was the real declaration of war in the Anglo-Boer conflict' and it was even more remarkable that Hawke took another team to South Africa in 1898–99, playing their last game only six months before war broke out.

All this is to digress. There was one area of common ground between those early tours and that of Hammond's party: long train journeys. Hawke's men could get no refreshment and the practice was to stop and purchase porridge at wayside stations, often too hot to consume before the train left. Hammond's men were well-fed and needed only to reconcile themselves to long hours in which there were considerable changes of altitude, great heat and frequent stops for water to meet the thirsty needs of the giant Garratt locomotives. Such a journey did the team make between the first Test at Johannesburg and the second at Cape Town, crossing the great Karoo Desert in a temperature of 145°F. At Cape Town Hammond played another very great innings, scoring 181 in five hours and sharing in a huge partnership with Ames. Balaskas, whose own 0 for 115 he ruefully recalled, had not forgotten the quality of Hammond's display and spoke of it with admiration.

Of all the grounds in the world on which Hammond played, Newlands, Cape Town, was the one he loved the best. He was not insensitive to beauty and colour. On Newlands ground nature has bestowed all her favours. The spectator may choose to look at play with the massive backcloth of Table Mountain skirting an entire length, its colour predominantly grey but changing in shadow and shade as the sun reaches and passes its northern zenith. Creeping like some hesitant caterpillar along a bank is an occasional train, its murmur attracting the ear rather than the eye. If you are lucky, you will see a grey squirrel casting a critical eye on the game as he hurries to his next destination.

A change of seat gives the spectator a view of massive oaks which are old enough to have seen and heard it all: the veld and pond cleared to make a ground; tea under the old pine trees for crino-lined ladies and their boatered escorts; sixes into Newlands Station; excursion trains from Cape Town at 7d first class; Bradman drinking Newlands' health in the Long Room but never playing there; Arthur Mailey pacifying an irate crowd with blackboard cartoons. The scene is completed by the green-roofed white pavilion and stand on one side and the new Memorial scoreboard and the Nursery on the other. Central to it all is the deep green turf on which play takes place. In the changing and turbulent scene which is the South Africa of the twentieth century, the ground at Newlands has been a continuing home of urbane tranquillity. Hammond would never play another innings at Newlands but he would return there nearly 30 years later under different, worthwhile and personally satisfying circumstances.

The Cape Town Test, like all the others, produced large scores on over-prepared wickets. Grass was replacing matting and groundsmen were preparing tracks which were plumb without pace, 'so far overstepping perfection as to be of little use to the bowler,' as the critic Robertson-Glasgow observed. Hammond himself was acutely aware of the problem: 'Bowlers on both sides could break their hearts and exercise every guile in the calendar, and still stand very little chance of getting a normally careful batsman out.' The effect of all this was to produce some tedious cricket which was relieved only by the attractive batting of Hammond himself, Paynter and the South Africa captain, Alan Melville. The first two were mainly responsible for England's huge score in the third Test at Durban which brought the only result in the series, an England win by an innings.

The brief visit to Rhodesia after the third Test had its curiosities both at Bulawayo and Salisbury. Neither ground had yet gone over to turf, while that at Bulawayo had no grass at all. White sand was used to dry the outfield, giving the impression of snow. At Salisbury, the clay which formed the base of the matting wicket was dried by lighted petrol, amid sheets of flame and black smoke. Despite these hazards – or counter-attractions – two matches took place.

Rain reduced prospects of a finish in the fourth Test and the two sides came together at Durban in a match designed to be played to a finish. The pleasant Kingsmead ground at Durban, with its bank of trees planted by individuals who had distinguished themselves there, became the scene of a game which has gone down in history as the Timeless Test. The Test at the Oval the previous September had shown the consequences of giving batsmen unlimited time but the lesson was not learnt until after this Durban game. The players went onto the field one Friday morning. In not the following week but the one after, they came off it for rain on a Tuesday. The contest was unfinished but abandoned.

To South Africa's 530, England replied with 316. A further 481 from South Africa left England 696 to win. In poor light on the evening of the sixth day, Hutton and P. A. Gibb set about a task which the South Africa press regarded as hopeless. Hammond knew he had a strong batting side and encouraged the attempt. By the evening of the seventh day, England had made 253 for the loss of Hutton. On day eight it rained and then came a Sunday. On the ninth scheduled day, England advanced to 496 for 3. A mere 200 were needed as Hammond and Paynter made the final assault on the tenth day. Rain punctuated their efforts. Hammond's 140 had been an innings of powerful drives and hits to leg and brought England within 40 runs of an incredible victory when a thunderstorm ended play. There could, of course, be an eleventh day – and indeed a twelfth – but the charade had to end. The night train for Cape Town left Durban at 8.05 pm. The boat home beckoned and the *Athlone Castle* could not delay its departure. MCC cabled to Hammond that they might consider bringing the party home by flying boat but after a conference between Hammond, his manager and the South Africa authorities, the decision was taken to end the match.

The Test had become a way of life to its participants. To Mitchell, the doyen of the South Africa side, 'it was like going to work every day.' Melville, the captain, recalled being woken up by the groundsman every morning at five o'clock for instructions. Even when the decision was Hammond's rather than Melville's, Melville had to take the call and relay it. 'Those five o'clock calls went on and on . . .' And the game went on and on for South Africa's wicket-keeper, R. E. Grieveson, and he liked it that way. He had batted for the first time in a Test, got himself what proved to be a Test career average of 57, stumped Hammond twice and simply enjoyed it all. Norman Gordon remembered bowling over 90 overs for a single wicket.

But the man of the match, long before such trophies were offered, was Bill Edrich. He was a gifted young cricketer, yet had a string of Test failures behind him both against the Australians in 1938 and on this tour. Hammond believed, with that shrewd judgement of technique and temperament in others which he had insufficient opportunity as captain or selector to display, that Edrich was a genuine Test player. What must have been his last chance came when Hammond selected him for the fifth Test and dispatched him to the wicket in the second innings charged with making a major contribution to the England target of 700. To a man who had compiled a mere 19 in all the Tests in the series, the prospect lay in the realms of fantasy. Had England needed 70, and he had been asked to get 20 of them, it would have been a realistic proposition. Hammond felt otherwise, encouraged the young man and told him when his first hundred came up at the end of the day to settle down and double it. That Edrich made 219 and became a peerless player in the post-war years owes much to Hammond's confidence and judgement as his captain.

Of Hammond's captaincy on that tour his opposite number, Melville, had a high regard. He admired his control of the fielders. 'They kept their eyes on him and responded to slight indications by eye or finger.' Others have suggested that Hammond learned much from the smooth self-assurance of the former captain of Oxford University and Sussex. As a pair, their contribution to a happy Test series was significant. They had far more to say to each other than Bradman and Hammond.

A more general judgement came from two journalists. E. W. Swanton, reporting the tour for the *Illustrated London News*, wrote that Hammond was 'a sagacious tactician' and displayed 'batting at its very best'. The historian of modern South African cricket, Louis Duffus, recorded:

> He maintained rigid discipline, set his field shrewdly, and was for ever besetting the batsmen with new strategies. Indeed, he introduced new methods to South African cricket by his policy of continually changing his attack and using his bowlers in short spells. He was an exemplary captain.

These accolades were supported by members of his own team. An incident during a match against one of the provincial sides reveals another aspect of Hammond's qualities as a leader besides reminding us of his physical strength. This is how one player remembered it:

> There was a good deal of rivalry between two fast bowlers, one on each side. They got into a quarrel off the field and a brawl was on the point of starting. Hammond stepped between these two angry giants, both fourteen stone, and simply pushed them apart. He dressed them down in a few well-chosen words, summoned the necessary drinks and restored good humour and harmony all round.

This was the gesture of a man in touch with his team and ready to anticipate any problems. Edrich remarked, 'He was the perfect leader, perceptive and astute on the field and an ambassador of the highest order off it.' Ames commented, 'No-one could have done the job better.' B. H. Valentine recalled that the tour owed everything to Hammond's light touch, personal humour and stupendous cricket. That 'stupendous cricket' had brought him a Test average of 87.00 and a tour average of 60.29.

The journey home gave time for reflection. Hammond felt content with his achievements on the field. Captaincy had proved no burden and his own playing standards had remained as high as ever. But in common with his colleagues, he was concerned about the course of events in Europe. The night the players had spent homeward bound in the train from Durban to Cape Town had been spent by Hitler in the ancient royal palace at Prague. Czechoslovakia had fallen. Newspapers, on the day the party boarded the *Athlone Castle*, carried reports of the speech of the British prime minister, Neville Chamberlain, on the implications of that event. Boat-drill on the ship was taken very seriously.

Hammond also had more personal matters to consider. In December 1938, he had met in Durban a young lady of great charm and attraction. Sybil Ness-Harvey had been beauty queen of Natal and it was her picture in the press which had caught his attention. She came of a well-known Natal family who had originally gone to South Africa in the nineteenth century. He took her as his escort to a reception given for the industrialist and philanthropist, Lord Nuffield, and they met again when MCC returned to Durban early in the New Year. From then onwards, in the view of one of the MCC party, 'his life centred on Sybil.'

Hammond's marriage to Dorothy had lasted nearly ten years. Her concern for him remained evident. We have seen how anxious she was to keep her illness secret during the 1936–37 MCC tour of Australia. His loyalties had been less evident, and he had from time to time looked elsewhere for female companionship. In 1937 he got to know the Wicks family. John and May Wicks lived at the Cedars, a Georgian house set in its own grounds in Thornbury, just a cricket ball's throw away from the village ground where W. G. Grace had played so often. Although the Wicks were family members of Gloucestershire County Cricket Club they did not press him to talk about the game, and he enjoyed the comfort and hospitality of their substantial home. Soon a serious friendship had developed between him and the Wicks's daughter,

Ursula, and they saw a lot of each other in the next 18 months. Then had come South Africa and Sybil Ness-Harvey.

Yet Dorothy had hoped the marriage would survive. Divorce was far less acceptable in the 1930s than it is now, as reaction to King Edward VIII's proposal to marry Mrs Simpson had shown. A married couple who no longer felt their marriage had been made in heaven would stay together. They would either work at it to achieve some degree of happiness or accept a relationship of convenience. Marriage remained the bourgeoisie convention. Dorothy's decision (with MCC approval) to go out to South Africa for the last part of the 1938–39 tour, when she had never previously travelled, may be seen as a positive gesture by her towards strengthening their marriage. Press photographs show her leaving by the boat train from London on 13 January 1939, smiling from her compartment window and armed with a bunch of flowers. Nearly three weeks later she joined her husband in Johannesburg. By then he had become deeply involved with the Durban girl who would eventually become his second wife. For those last six weeks of the tour, obligation and inclination jostled for position in the private life of the England cricket captain.

The West Indians were the visitors in 1939. They found themselves against an England side which had amassed a series of large totals in the previous ten months. While England had averaged 640 for a completed innings in that time, their opponents, Australia and South Africa, had averaged 351. This was the measure of England's batting strength that summer. It was to the credit of the West Indies that they lost only one Test out of three and suffered no discredit in drawing the other two. The comparison of figures may be taken further. England's average of runs per wicket for the series was 45.8 while that of the West Indies was 26.7. Statistically, the West Indians would perform marginally better than had England's two other opponents in the ten months before the first Test at Lord's in June 1939.

Hammond secured an England victory in the three days allotted to the match, declaring England's first innings closed with nice judgement and using a well-balanced attack to best advantage. A classic off-drive by the captain won the game for England but it had really been an occasion for the young players of the future, Hutton and Compton, to score memorable centuries. Thunderclouds of various kinds hung over the match. The conventional type threatened to end play, while appeals over the loudspeaker were made by Hammond for men to volunteer for national service in preparation for the imminent war with Germany. The *Daily Mail* cartoonist, Tom Webster, depicted the match as 'Winter Sports', so cold and dark were conditions on the second day of play. Some people felt that sport itself would soon be at a premium.

Hammond, in common with others in public positions, was involved in recruiting throughout the summer. He had no illusions about war and its implications: as a schoolboy he had been called to the headmaster's study to be told his father had been killed on the Western Front. But he believed that Britain had no option other than to meet the threat of Hitler to the peace and stability of Europe.

The second Test at Old Trafford was spoilt by cold, rain and bad light. Hammond made two declarations when England's score was 164 and 128 but too much time was lost to get a result. Of his loud-speaker appeals for volunteers from Manchester to join the Forces, Constantine commented, 'He was addressing the right stuff, for only the lion-hearted remained to watch in the appalling conditions.' Constantine, too, was aware of the increasing tension and wrote this compelling description of the atmosphere surrounding the last Test at the Oval:

> Over the Oval ground hung silvery shapes of cruel omen – barrage balloons flying in case the German bombers should drone overhead during the match and make an unheralded murder attack on London at play. There was the drone of flying to be heard, unusual in London then; khaki and naval blue and a sprinkling of Air Force uniforms showed everywhere among the crowds; as we approached the Oval I saw gunners ostentatiously moving an anti-aircraft gun by means of a tractor. Later we were told that this was strategy to deceive German spies into mistaking London's four guns for a large number. There was feverish hurry at the stations, and despite the glorious sunshine, one saw hard and frightened faces. August 1939, Test match cricket – and Death hovering in the air with a shadow everywhere.

The game itself left the spectators with memories to savour in the grim years which followed. Constantine's own batting gave them gaiety, exuberance and that carefree attitude which had made him such a box-office attraction in League cricket. Hammond set a spread-eagled field with no slips but nothing could stop Constantine's onslaught until he was caught by Arthur Wood, the wicket-keeper, running back almost to the pavilion. Hammond and Hutton put on 264 for the third wicket in England's second innings. With a century, Hammond exceeded Bradman's number of Test centuries. One of those who observed Hammond at close quarters in those Tests was the 18-year-old Jeffrey Stollmeyer, a future captain of the West Indies. Hammond's batting, he thought, was 'a picture of grace and power' and 'his knowledge of the game and his tactics could not be faulted.'

Hammond as a player had achieved all that was demanded of him and as a captain had fulfilled the expectations of those who had appointed him in the 12 Tests in which he led England before the war. Nor had Gloucestershire's needs been forgotten. In 1939 he had taken over the county captaincy and, said *Wisden*, 'set a fashion in enterprising cricket and a spirit of adventure which made Gloucestershire second to none as an attraction.' Yet there still lingers the criticism that he lacked the qualities of leadership when young players needed encouragement. Gloucestershire were playing Kent at Maidstone in one of the last games of the summer. Wickets had fallen cheaply, including Hammond's own. The young man sitting next to him, a Cambridge Blue of the year making his county debut, was in. Not a word of advice or encouragement was given as he set forth. The individual was left to prove himself. Hammond led by example rather than by guidance, and huge scores by him against Warwickshire, Kent and Essex paved the way for massive victories.

That successful Gloucestershire XI gathered together for the last time for six years a few days after the final Test. Barnett and Hammond gave a Saturday afternoon crowd at Trent Bridge something to remember, scoring 81 and 153 respectively. Other stalwarts of the 1930s were there: Billy Neale, Hammond's old Cirencester school friend, and Reg Sinfield. Goddard collected 11 wickets and Gloucestershire ended their season third in the Championship.

The man who had dominated the English cricket scene between the wars and had achieved the game's greatest rewards had played almost 600 first-class matches. He had become a hero and an idol to countless Englishmen. He had performed in an age when entertainment was a foil to the Depression and escapism an antidote to the dictators. Thousands had watched him.

They had flocked to the cinema for similar reasons, finding relief and excitement in the celluloid stars of Hollywood. They gazed at these larger-than-life figures – remote, unapproachable, talented, groomed, elegant.

Hammond's brilliance, matched by his finely chiselled features, well-cut clothes and fast cars, gave him the qualities of stardom. For women he had the attraction of a Rudolph Valentino. His name was constantly in the papers, instantly recognisable. When Movietone News portrayed a piece of cricket, the star of the cricket field became one with the stars of Hollywood.

Stars lived in the public glare. Autograph-hunters besieged them, fans mobbed them, gossip-columnists plagued them. The actors – the real ones or the cricketing ones – were on stage all the time. Appearances mattered. Artificial smiles were manufactured to meet the public demand. But a protective shell formed and they retreated behind this into some sort of privacy; into a life which had some vestige of normality, in which ordinary things happened. There was variety in the way in which they coped with their stardom. The actress, Joan Crawford, was so completely the star that her whole existence was committed to the role. Fantasy blended with reality to create one personality. The private moments of some stars of comedy were tinged with sadness.

How did Hammond react to the role? Part of him enjoyed the adulation of the crowd. He paused, some would say, to savour its applause before going in to bat. But he liked it to remain a faceless multitude. The crowd at close quarters he found uncomfortable. 'I suffered from hero-worship. I know it was offered in all kindness but it embarrassed.'

His reaction may be explained both in terms of his personality and of his views on team spirit. Hammond the individual found the proximity of the hero-worshipper awkward. He could (though by no means always) spurn the autograph-hunter, turn aside the conversationalist at some party, remain, like the celluloid stars, remote and unapproachable. This was his way. Hammond the cricketer put team before self and collective performance before individual goals. He wrote, 'Personal outstanding achievements are all right, and the whole team is unselfishly proud of the man who attains them. But those who are fortunate enough to win big success owe more than the public ever realises to the great-hearted co-operation of others. It most certainly was so in anything I would be fortunate enough to do.' The thread of personal modesty ran constantly through his career. He was the reluctant star.

8
Squadron Leader, 1939–45

'The great attraction, comparable
to W.G., Jessop and Ranji'.
The Times, 1944

In the months before the second world war Hammond had
identified himself with the recruiting campaign and his fellow-
directors at Marsham Tyres were not in the least surprised when
he announced that he was joining up. He was commissioned as a
pilot officer in the RAFVR in October 1939 and posted as a super-
numary officer to No. 3 Initial Training Wing at Hastings in Sussex,
moving with it to Torquay in the following year. At the end of 1940
he was sent abroad.

His duties were of an administrative and routine nature. Members of 'C' Squadron recalled him inspecting them every morning
on the sea-front and putting men on charges for dirty buttons. Had
he been playing cricket against Sussex he might have thought
about the atmospheric effect on the ball. The connection between
the salty atmosphere and corrosion on buttons escaped him. He
was, in a word, tough with young aircrew recruits, many of whom
would shortly be commissioned and fight in the Battle of Britain.
'My schoolboy idol crashed before my very eyes,' said one service-
man of those days.

But Hammond was not there to keep alive the spirit of hero-
worship. His role was to lead these men to become heroes themselves and to make discipline, however irksome, an axiom in their
daily existence. His authoritarian attitude won fewer critics than

admirers. 'At the end of an ITW course we respected the officers who knocked us into shape. Hammond was the ideal choice,' one officer wrote. The warrant officer with whom he worked, Bill Hill, was a man in his forties with a lifetime of RAF service behind him. Hill appreciated the not-so-young pilot officer and had no doubt that 'he was concerned to do his best for the cadets.' Their commanding officer, Group Captain Jack Butterworth, had played representative Service rugby and cricket and had specially secured Hammond's posting to the Wing. He had no reason to regret his judgement, especially in the summer of 1940 when cricket was arranged for the airmen.

Cricket flourished to a surprising degree during the second world war. In contrast to the prevailing view taken in 1914 that it was unpatriotic to play, the game was offered to the public as entertainment and as a way of helping war charities, and to the players as relaxation. In Sir Pelham Warner's view, 'If Goebbels had been able to broadcast that the war had stopped cricket at Lord's, it would have been valuable propaganda for the Germans.' The different ways in which the two wars were conducted also contributed to the change of attitude. Men in the first world war were for the most part in trenches in Europe or serving at sea. In the second, there was no occupation of Europe between the Dunkirk retreat in 1940 and the invasion of Italy in 1943. Large numbers of troops were being mobilised in Britain, and the RAF throughout the war operated from stations in the British Isles. Operational pilots and their crews might play cricket in the intervals between night raids on Germany. Wartime cricket was stimulated by the foundation of two clubs, the British Empire XI and London Counties. Both of these sides played a large number of matches for charity. The first-class counties were content to stage only an occasional match.

Hammond did not appear in 1940 for either of the newly formed clubs. His first game was at Lewes in May for an RAF XI v. Sussex. He and Ames were the only famous names though the golfer L. G. Crawley, an Essex cricketer, also played. Hammond's 63 was the principal feature of the day and a press photograph showed him, immaculate as ever, hair centrally parted and cut short in service fashion, smilingly signing autographs. The dismissal of one player produced an entry unique in cricket history: 'c. Hammond, b. Ames'. Later in the summer when some dozen one-day games took place at Lord's, Hammond was far away in

Torquay. Instead, he organised cricket for others and played in a match at Torquay between 'Stars' and 'the Rest of Devon'. During the tea interval news came through that one of the 'Stars', Edrich, had successfully completed his flying training. In his excitement, he jumped up and scattered a bowl of Devonshire cream all over Hammond. Edrich was to have a distinguished war record as a bomber pilot.

Just after Christmas 1940, Hammond was posted to RAF Middle East Headquarters at Cairo which remained his parent unit until Christmas 1943. During his three years in Africa, in what was a 'Special Duties' posting, he was responsible for promoting sporting facilities for the officers and men serving there. His brief was wide and extended to the authorisation of finance for entertainments and sports equipment. As an example of this, he funded the purchase of musical instruments at an RAF unit at George on the south of the Cape – the band thus formed toured service stations and broadcast to the Forces. His appointment, in the rank of flight lieutenant and subsequently squadron leader, suited him admirably. His was not a war in which he had to face the enemy with the courage of, say, Bill Edrich or the sacrifice of Hedley Verity and Kenneth Farnes. Cynics might say that he had a 'soft' war and in some ways they would be right. But High Command decides what men will do in war and the judgement of Hammond's war service must be made not on what he did, but on the way he did it. The harsher qualities which he had felt necessary with recruits in 1939 were not displayed. He was, in the view of colleagues of all ranks, thoroughly acceptable as a person and efficient as an officer.

The actual cricket which he played overseas began in an unusual way. On leaving Britain, he had landed at the port of Takoradi on the Gold Coast where the RAF had a large unit to assemble planes brought from England by sea. That day the unit were due to play the gold-mining township of Tarkwa, and Hammond was asked to make a guest appearance in the closing overs. In borrowed kit, straight from an English December, he went to the wicket in steaming heat and scored 44 not out in the few minutes left before the sun fell.

A week later his transport to Cairo had still not arrived and he played for the RAF against Sekondi. This, to the RAF, was the contest that mattered. Sekondi had always seemed invincible. Hammond was instructed to take no risks! Going in at no. 3, he took the occasion seriously, picked the right ball to hit and eventually reached 94 before being caught on the boundary by a catch which was a talking-point for the Sekondi spectators for years to come.

Next morning he flew off. The airmen in that remote station had had a good week. He had played with them twice and coached them in the evenings. The game in the Gold Coast, as in Egypt, had been established by the presence of British administrators, businessmen and service personnel. In Egypt especially, there was a tradition going back nearly a century and in the decade before 1939 a touring side had gone to Egypt annually.

Cairo was an excellent place at which to be stationed. Hotels such as Shepherd's offered the best in food and wine. The Gezira Club met the needs of golfers and cricketers. Outdoor cinemas provided evening entertainment. At times war could seem very far away, but crises could suddenly bring it alarmingly near. The war brought to Middle East Command in Egypt many top-class players in various sports and Hammond found himself playing in the company of old opponents such as Dudley Nourse and Athol Rowan. One of his best performances was in August 1941 when he made a century for the Gezira Club against the South African Infantry Brigade. Numerous letters have testified to the friendly manner in which Hammond played his cricket in Egypt. A destroyer from the Mediterranean Fleet limped, heavily damaged, into Alexandria. During repairs, the crew played a few games and one rating recalled Hammond quietly coaching him from first slip while he batted. Another rating asked Hammond to bat wearing his own naval cap, which he duly did. One RAF man found himself keeping wicket to the great man's bowling. After he had dropped a couple of catches and felt himself going to pieces, Hammond came up with 'Never mind, lad, you're not the only 'keeper to have dropped a catch off my bowling.' A Scots NCO recalled the nervousness with which he approached captaining a side with Hammond in it and was given confidence and encouragement. Finally, a more unusual occasion was at the small RAF unit of Helouan where he was persuaded to turn out as A. N. Other but his cover was blown within a few minutes of coming to the crease!

During 1941 the North African campaign had suffered some reverses. Wavell, who had made (in Churchill's words) 'an important contribution to our final success', was replaced by Auchinleck. The defence of Tobruk against a German invasion of

Egypt was vital. Yet in the midst of this serious situation, the army and naval commanders-in-chief dispatched the best cricketers from the British and Australian Forces by sea from Tobruk to Egypt for a 'Test' match at Cairo. Hammond, as many have recalled, made the occasion a memorable one. Those who played and those who watched were given something to sustain them in the days ahead. Air Marshal Sir Anthony Selway believed Hammond's cricketing performances at the Gezira Club did a great deal for the morale of troops on leave from the campaign against Rommel in the Western Desert.

There is an obvious risk of over-dramatising his contribution, but for those who enjoyed playing and watching cricket, his influence was tremendous. For those whom the game passed by, such as his own room-mate in Cairo, there were other diversions. The room-mate was an RAF Medical Officer with no interest in or knowledge of the game at all, who would blandly inquire, tongue in cheek, what exactly it was that Hammond had done for a living before the war.

On one occasion in 1941 Hammond's duties took him to Kenya, an event described in the official history of the Kenya Kongonis Cricket Club by its historian, Clifford Braimbridge:

> A special Charity Match was arranged between the Club and Southern Rhodesian Armoured Car Regiment which put quite a strong side into the field, and everything was perfect. The sun shone, the grass was green, never before had so many spectators congregated at a cricket match in Kenya and lastly but most importantly Hammond scored a typical and chanceless hundred. He played on one or two other occasions during this and other visits and by his modesty and charm made himself deservedly popular with all who met him.

Kenya was a staging-point for South Africa, where he spent much of the latter part of his overseas posting. There he continued to take his share in unit fixtures. More important was the one first-class match in which he took part. In December 1942 he captained an RAF XI brought in from all the units stationed in South Africa against the Rest of South Africa in a three-day match at Johannesburg. His own contribution was 60 in a match which a powerful Rest XI won by five wickets.

Many times, as part of his wide brief throughout the continent of Africa, he flew the tedious Sunderland flying-boat passage from Cairo to the Cape with stops at Khartoum, Lake Victoria, Mombasa,

Lake Nyasa and Durban. Whenever possible, he took his leave in Durban, where he renewed his friendship with Sybil Ness-Harvey. The circumstances of war had charted a course for him. The friendship with Ursula Wicks, which had flourished just before the war and had been sustained in 1940, withered with his departure abroad. Her home at Thornbury had been a pleasant place to go on leave. But Sybil supplanted her in his affections and an understanding was reached between them: when the war was over, she would come to England and he would set about ending his marriage with Dorothy. That marriage had now become a forlorn thing. In the parlance of a later age, the marriage floundered through incompatibility. Possibly Dorothy made the greater effort to save it, but her reluctance to have children made the relationship vulnerable. Their home had been sold up and Dorothy had gone to live in the Isle of Wight, sometimes visiting his mother. Later she returned to the north of England and passed forever out of his life. He was not an insensitive man, and the eventual dissolution of their marriage caused him some tension, as we shall see, when he captained England in the first post-war series. His relationship with Sybil was scarcely a wartime romance in the accepted sense since they had met before it. Nevertheless, out of their renewed meeting in the war came their subsequent marriage and, in the last two decades of his life, a personal happiness which had eluded him hitherto.

In January 1944, Hammond returned to England and was posted to No. 3 Aircrew Reception Centre in Regent's Park. His office was in a requisitioned flat in St John's Wood, his mess was in Winfield House, Regent's Park, the former home of the Woolworth's heiress, Barbara Hutton, and his duties took him to Lord's. The practice area and the buildings around Lord's had been requisitioned by the RAF, and there he took his turn in lecturing to aircrew cadets on Air Force Law. He and his fellow flight-commanders would march men down St John's Wood Road to the zoo in Regent's Park where they would drill and where the airmen's mess was situated. 'Watching us cadets eat in the restaurant appealed to the crowds as much as the animals,' one cadet of those days remembered. The squadron leader of 1944 made fewer demands than the pilot officer of 1940. A fellow flight-commander was 'proud to have known such a likeable person'. Another one recalled 'an affable person' and a trivial incident of some humour: Hammond wanted a cigarette lighter and asked for it to be thrown across a large room. The owner hesitated. 'Don't worry, I'll catch it' was the reassuring comment. 'Bravely, I threw my lighter . . . and he caught it.' His catching also took the eye of another colleague whose ignorance of cricket was profound. Once taken to see Hammond play, he saw him make a catch and recorded 'a terrific catch at slips, I believe it is called, which was made to look ever so casual.'

His return to England meant that he could play a great deal of cricket in 1944. Indeed, his posting to Regent's Park and his lecturing at Lord's could be described as 'living above the shop', for the cricket ground there saw him almost as often on Saturdays as the Nursery area did on working days. 'His return,' said the London *Evening Standard*, 'was the best piece of news cricketers have had for a long time and everyone hopes he will lead England when the Tests are resumed. He should have many more years of good cricket.' This was the prevailing view and nothing Hammond did in 1944, or for that matter in 1945 or 1946, hinted that his career would end so abruptly in March 1947.

His arrival in England coincided with the decision to stage even more major matches at Lord's than previously. Charity, the public and the players themselves gained from such occasions and five games were arranged for 1944. The Royal Australian Air Force styled itself 'Australia' and although the label was somewhat grandiose, the performances of the side were ample justification. England, the West Indies, the Rest (of the World) and the Dominions were the other contestants. The one-day games took place at the Whitsun and August Bank Holiday weekends or on Saturdays. They often attracted crowds of over 20,000 and over £4000 was raised for various charities. The admission charge of one shilling (5p) puts into context the great amount by which charities benefited. On Whit Monday, when England played Australia, the crowd reached over 30,000. Half an hour before play began, the queue outside encircled the entire ground and the gates were closed at 12.30. The matches were broadcast and the press reports lengthy. 'England win at Lord's' was a banner headline in *The Times*. There were no concessions such as 'an England XI' or indeed 'an Australian (Air Force) XI'.

One might be forgiven for thinking the war was over. Not so: momentous things were happening in Europe. The Allies landed in France on D-Day, 6 June, and the vast sweep through Europe began. Those who had doubted the eventual outcome of the war were converted. Total victory seemed imminent and, as a symbol of that hope, people could once again take their holidays at the beaches. Others continued the wartime policy of holidays at home which, for some, meant playing or watching cricket. A fair wind blew and sometimes, as when England played Australia, the sun blazed. But all was not fair and the realities of a continuing conflict were brought home in a number of ways. Three days after England beat the West Indies at Lord's (Hammond 100) the first flying bomb fell on London. Within a month a million and a half people were evacuated and 6000 of those who stayed in London were killed. When the RAF played the Army at Lord's in July, a flying bomb seemed almost certain to hit the ground. Players flung themselves to the ground, Hammond included, but the bomb fell in Regent's Park. Jack Robertson relieved the tension by hitting a six from the first ball after the resumption.

The realities of war were emphasised a few days after the Whitsun games. Australia's opening bat, W. A. Roach, a flight sergeant, was reported missing in an operation over Germany and his death was later confirmed. A second player from that game, the captain, D. K. Carmody, a Beaufort pilot in Coastal Command, was also reported missing over the Dutch coast. Subsequently he was found to be a prisoner of war. Just a year later he was back in England and playing in the second Victory match for Australia against England – as was R. G. Williams, four years a prisoner but still fit and able to claim Hutton's wicket four times in the series.

Hammond played in all five of the 'great matches' at Lord's – to use the term beloved of nineteenth-century writers. He scored 252 runs for an average of 50.40, making two centuries while (with 1 and 0) disappointing the crowd on two other occasions. *Wisden*, incorrectly, described him as making his first wartime appearance in England when he led the Rest against Australia and made 46. *The Times* said that 'no two teams could have risen to the occasion more nobly' and praised Hammond for a declaration which made a close and dramatic result possible. His single for England against Australia left others to get the runs. England did so and won by six wickets, but their side contained eight Test players and the Australian side none. The performance of the Australians was a pointer not only to the Victory series in 1945 but also to the tour in 1946–47. In the third contest England vanquished the West Indies. Hammond and Constantine, old rivals, were the opposing captains. Both won ovations from the crowd for their batting,

Hammond's 'carefree disposition delighting the spectators and confounding the bowlers'. His greatest personal performance came in the August game against Australia. He gave a classic display of driving in a century which left no-one in doubt that he was aching for the resumption of Test cricket and a chance to play the 'real' Australians.

He was also available to captain the RAF side. Their matches raised over £3000 for the RAF Benevolent Fund and took him to various parts of the country, so that he appeared on several county grounds for the first time for five years. The old Somerset player, Bill Andrews, has recalled playing with him at Worcester:

> I had my chit to report to the Hopmarket Hotel, Worcester, the evening before the match. Rather uneasily, I approached the dining room to have a meal. I began to push the door open and I saw the only occupant was Hammond, sitting on his own in the corner. I began quietly to retreat but he spotted me and called me over to join him. What sort of a reception would I get, joining him alone for a meal? He never stopped talking and, for a change, I was an attentive listener.
>
> Yet in the dressing room next morning, not a single word from Wally. We won the toss, put Worcestershire in to bat, and he threw the ball to me. Our skipper gave me slips and a gully for the left-hander and a leg trap for the right-hander. Of course, I made a hopeless mess of it. The ball started swinging the wrong way.
>
> After an over, Hammond switched the fielders to the other side of the wickets – and then I found myself bowling inswingers. It was awful. I could see the skipper's face and that was enough. After four overs, he glowered at me and said, 'Put your sweater on.'

Andrews had seen this shy, sometimes morose man relax and talk. He had also seen the stern, unspoken appraisal of a man's performance which could be part of Hammond's make-up.

Being back in England meant a chance to renew old friendships. One evening he called on Freddie Mills, whom he had known since his schooldays at Cirencester. His wife, Florence, great-great-great-granddaughter of Flora Macdonald, the heroine of the Jacobite 'Rebellion' of 1745, chatted to me below a portrait of her ancestor whom she strikingly resembled. She was proud to be in her late nineties, to be a Highlander and to be a cricket enthusiast. ('My brothers used to tell me to get my feet right,' she told me. It was the same advice Tunnicliffe had given to the young Hammond.) She had watched the game over the decades and found Hammond 'wonderful to watch'. Through her husband, she got to know him. 'I made him argue. I wouldn't let him be silent and shy! I felt I had achieved something when he said to me, "You're an obstinate and high-handed woman." I just replied that I was a Highlander and what did he expect.'

Her husband agreed that it was quite a feat to make Hammond angry. It was also a feat to get him to display happiness. Only when among a few friends, as Leslie Ames recalled, 'might he sometimes be on top of the world.' In contrast, there were occasions when he would seem depressed and moody. Friends and colleagues kept their distance until his manner changed. It was, indeed, just as Bill Andrews had seen in that game at Worcester.

Other matches in that summer of 1944 included a rain-ruined one at Leeds as a memorial to Hedley Verity, a Festival game (wartime style) at Scarborough and a match against the West of England XI at Gloucester where he was dismissed for 69 by his old county colleague, Sinfield – who thus added the scalp of Hammond to that of Bradman six years earlier. The West of England XI, another wartime club, prevailed on him to play for them in one match at Clifton College when, *rara dies*, he dropped two catches at first slip off successive balls. He finished the season with an impressive record:

Innings	N.O.	Runs	H.S.	Ave.
14	2	754	117	62.83

But figures tell only part of the tale. He had given a glamour to wartime cricket it had hitherto lacked. At the end of the season one journalist, Robin Baily, summed it up:

> Throughout a long and exciting history no cricketer has done so much for our incomparable game in such a short time as Hammond has this summer, with consummate ease and the enchantments of a stylist.

The popularity of this one-day cricket at the highest level and Hammond's own performance in it prompt three questions. Why was it so popular? Was it considered as a prospect for the post-war era? How did Hammond himself react to it?

The immediate popularity and the huge crowds need little explanation. As we have seen, wartime 'escapism' and relaxation, the prospect of seeing a finish in one day and the public delight in cricket being available as a major spectacle were all important factors. Trevor Bailey recalled the excitement of those games in which he had played as a young man: 'People simply wanted to play and watch cricket after so many years of war.'

As early as December 1942 an Advisory Committee had been appointed by MCC to consider the future of the game after the war. Its composition was of administrators rather than players and its average age was high. The way its deliberations were likely to go was hinted at by Sir Pelham Warner in his speech, as president, at the Middlesex AGM that year:

> I can see nothing wrong with modern cricket except there are too many counties and some wickets are over-prepared and over-doped. Do not be led away by the call for bright cricket. It is a leisurely, intricate game of skill. We live in an age of speed and people are apt to think that cricket must be speeded up; but my experience is that it is not necessary to have fast scoring to have interesting cricket. I do not wish to see anything better than two fine batsmen opposed to two first-class bowlers, backed up by good fielding; then the number of runs scored in an hour is unimportant.

The Committee in principle favoured three-day cricket – and recalled the failure of two-day cricket in 1919 – but delegated detailed planning to a Select Committee, under the chairmanship of Sir Stanley Jackson, which met between November 1943 and March 1944. County captains figured largely in its composition, one of those who contributed to the debate being the Glamorgan captain, M. J. Turnbull, who was killed in action in the Normandy landings shortly afterwards. Hammond, posted back to England in December 1943, joined the committee after its first meeting. Among those called to give evidence were Ames, the umpire Frank Chester, Leyland and the old Surrey wicket-keeper, Herbert Strudwick. It could be fairly said that the Select Committee represented or drew upon a broad basis of opinion from those closely involved in the game.

The report of the Jackson Committee ran to 6000 words. In essence, it was a conservative document recommending changes of a minimal nature and none which affected either the number of counties playing or the length of matches. Groundsmen were instructed to prepare fast wickets and there was concern at the extent to which they had been 'doped' before the war. The appeal of the Findlay Commission of 1937 for attacking cricket was re-iterated: 'The team shall aim for victory from the first ball and maintain an enterprising attitude towards the game until the last ball is bowled.' Finally, the committee recommended that the possibility of a knock-out competition (of three-day matches) be investigated 'while we see many practical difficulties in the proposals.' A sub-committee, of which Hammond was not a member, put forward such a plan early in 1945 which the original Select Committee, meeting again in the summer of 1945, referred back for further consideration. In 1946 the plan was deferred *sine die*. Cricket in the post-war world would continue in the same guise as it had since the turn of the century. Ten years went by before the Altham Committee in 1956 made the first proposals for a one-day knock-out competition, eventually to make its appearance in 1963.

So far as administrators and players were concerned, the one-day game had not come into their deliberations between 1943 and 1945 despite the popular support it was enjoying. The war-time one-day game differed in some important ways from that pioneered in the 1960s. The major distinction lay in the concept of limited-overs cricket. Part of the appeal of the earlier one-day game lay in the clever timing of declarations. It was indeed 'good, clean fun'. Who won was of no great moment providing a wartime crowd was entertained. A good finish might in fact be a drawn match. That extra dimension, an exciting draw, remains today a feature of one-day friendly cricket or, as the Australians call it, social cricket. But none of this could apply when one-day cricket became competitive. At stake were cups, trophies and prize-money such as no pre-war county cricketer ever visualised in his most extravagant dreams. Someone had to win and someone had to lose. When limited-overs cricket was eventually adopted, as E. W. Swanton has written in his *Barclays World of Cricket*, it 'not only proved a financial necessity but [gave] a vast deal of pleasure to a wider public both present at the games and, of course, watching on television.'

The one-day game as it was played with great enjoyment in the war years could have no future in a professional, commercial cricket world, as Elton Ede pointed out in the *Sunday Times*:

> The thousands who have thronged Lord's this last month have indeed been lucky in the cricket provided in exchange for their shillings. Risks have been accepted, tea intervals abolished, and, best of all, games have see-sawed their way to a climax of excitement and reached a decision instead of fizzling tamely out into a draw.
>
> So, if one took the equivalent of a Gallup poll from the present

cricket-watching public, it would perhaps show a decided majority in favour of one-day matches, not merely for the present but also for the future. The spectators would say, with truth, that the 1944 brand of one-day cricket seemed to them a good deal brighter and more alive than the pre-war three-day matches. This is, however, a testimony to the spirit in which cricket is now being played rather than to one-day matches.

We see a sporting declaration, and the side which declares loses. At the moment they are praised – but would the supporters of a County praise their own captain for giving away several matches in the course of a season? Would this light-hearted chivalry appeal to Yorkshire and Lancashire? The question has only to be asked to be answered. One-day matches are just a jolly war-time expedient for the full rigour of the game.

Thirdly, how did Hammond himself react? That he entered thoroughly into the spirit of those one-day games won testimony from the editor of *Wisden* in the 1945 edition who called him 'Hammond the Sportsman'. He praised him for his declarations which made exciting finishes possible and for dispensing with the tea interval to increase the likelihood of a result. Editorial praise was also conferred upon his decision, when the RAF played the Army at Bradford, to have a new wicket cut after rain and so make cricket possible. The editor's concluding comment was, 'After all, people want to play and see cricket, and providing nothing unfair is done, surely such a thing as moving the pitch helps to keep the game alive and sends the crowd home happy instead of disappointed.'

Hammond himself was the great attraction, 'comparable to WG, Jessop and Ranji,' wrote *The Times*, and he responded to the public. Press reports repeatedly described him in words such as 'getting the best out of the one-day game', 'the highlight of the match' and 'realising that sixes were the most profitable stroke'. All this evidence – cancelling tea intervals and hitting sixes with abandon – confirms the view that he saw those games for what they were: delightful expedients which had no place in the first-class game. His own contribution to the discussions of the Select Committee had been firmly on the side of the game returning to what it had been in 1939. Sir Pelham Warner, who was joint secretary of the Select Committee, has left on record his view of Hammond's shrewdness and soundness at its meetings: 'He was a man who knew his own mind and could argue a point of view.'

Yet his approach in 1944 does him credit. He enjoyed his cricket in a relaxed way, had less need to concentrate and communicated his enjoyment to others. It was total concentration in the sterner struggles which had played a part in his successful career. Wicket-keepers such as Oldfield have testified that they could get no small talk out of him between overs or when wickets fell.

Hammond's war ended on 22 December 1944 when he was discharged from the RAFVR on health grounds. He was entitled to retain the rank of squadron leader on relinquishing his commission. The fibrositis which within three years would end his first-class cricket career was a cause of increasing concern. Curiously, two other contemporaries of his, Bradman and Hutton, were both discharged from the services on medical grounds and their prospects of playing after the war were in doubt.

Within days Hammond was back with Marsham Tyres, picking up the threads of his role as their outside 'contacts' man and sharing in the firm's plans for post-war expansion in some dozen new branches. His particular colleague of the pre-war years, Bill Pope, took over as managing director and the two men worked closely in dealing with problems raised by the continuation of Tyre Control, even after the war was over, and by changed trading conditions. When they discussed where expansion might – and did – take place, Hammond was closely involved and again showed in the board room and in a different area of post-war planning the shrewdness which Warner had observed in the Select Committee. He was also concerned in the business of selling surplus war stocks of tyres to overseas markets and in the establishment of Pneumatics (Overseas) Ltd, the subsidiary of Marsham Tyres set up to handle these exports. Links were established with Europe, the United States and the African Continent. Those with the Union of South Africa (which he visited on business in 1948) were to become important in his own later career.

He was still a man on the right side of middle age. Men a little younger than he had to establish themselves for the first time after the war, sometimes going up to University first. He had the advantage of some pre-war business experience and, with the immense prestige which attached to his name, the prospects for his future were favourable. A long business career might have lain in front of him as it did for Bill Pope. In 1983, nearly 40 years after the war, Pope was still an energetic businessman long past retiring age but in demand as a consultant in the tyre industry all over the world.

The war in Europe ended on 8 May 1945. The authorities at Lord's were obviously unable to restore a full first-class programme at such short notice but five three-day matches were arranged between England and Australia. They were not intended to be Test matches and were never scheduled as such. In the mood of the moment, they were called 'Victory' matches. Australia raised their side from servicemen brought back from Europe and the Middle East. A. L. Hassett was the only Test cricketer in the party, although Keith Miller quickly gave notice of post-war intentions. No other player became a Test cricketer, but in beating a near-representative England XI in the first game, the side indicated the depth of Australian cricket. England got their revenge at Sheffield on a bomb-scarred Bramall Lane. Hammond's century on a turning wicket, delaying his stroke off the back foot until the last possible minute, was the centre-piece of the game and he turned four sharp chances at slip into catches made to look easy. He described his own innings as 'one of the most satisfactory' of his career. Lumbago was his master in the third game, 'the remorseless shadow'. Half-centuries came his way in the fourth and fifth games and again there were slip catches which took everyone's breath away.

Two unrelated incidents are reminders that the context of war remained close. Thousands of miles away from the fifth Victory game at Old Trafford, E. W. Swanton, walking out of his Japanese prisoner of war camp as a free man, came upon a wireless set in a Thai village outside the camp. He tuned in and picked up the commentary from the ground. The other was at Old Trafford itself, where the pavilion was being repainted by German prisoners of war. Paid at the rate of three-farthings an hour (£0.003 per hour), they can scarcely have become converts to the game.

But the real show-piece of that 1945 season came at the end of August in a match between England and the Dominions. The captains were Hammond and Constantine. The editor of *Wisden* echoed many other observers when he called it 'one of the finest games ever produced'. The match belonged to Miller with a dazzling, swift and faultless 185; to Wright with five wickets in each innings; to the New Zealander, Martin Donnelly, for a century; to J. G. W. Davies, the man who once bowled Bradman as an undergraduate, for a fighting fifty at the end; to Constantine as a black captain leading ten white men and fielding with all his old brilliance; to Hammond for making a century in each innings and becoming the first man to do so seven times; to the two captains whose strategy and attitudes set up such a great match. This is how Hammond described the game from the moment when Constantine ran out W. E. Phillipson:

> One of the finest returns I have ever been thrilled to see: to be held up as pure Constantine amidst generations of cricketers yet to come. That was almost the end of us. We still needed 45 when our last wicket went down. Who cared! It was one of the grandest matches I have ever taken part in, swift, strenuous, with thrilling changes of fortune.

In a sense, that great game was the swan-song of wartime cricket. Japan surrendered that week and VJ Day was celebrated on 2 September 1945, six years less a day since the war had begun. The historian, A. J. P. Taylor, has argued that the war was primarily fought for the destruction of Hitler and National Socialism. Hammond, a soldier's son, had seen it that way as well. To him, Hitler and his policies represented aggression and tyranny. He wrote, 'Now, after years in the shadows, England was emerging into the sunshine again.'

9
Post-War Duty, 1946–51

'See him while you can'.
Picture Post, 1946

The Parks, Oxford, May 1946: in that splendid setting of a ground within a ground, surrounded by a wide variety of trees, graced by a Victorian pavilion with gables and a cupola and flanked by the distant roofs of North Oxford houses, Hammond and Gloucester-shire renewed the craft of first-class cricket in a peace-time context. Some of the undergraduates, elderly by normal standards, were ex-servicemen. One, M. P. Donnelly, was a pre-war New Zealand Test player. But their years did not match those of Goddard who took nine of their wickets nor of Hammond who scored 103. (A future Provost of Eton toiled that day to take 0 for 100.)

Then at the Gloucester Railway Carriage and Wagon Company ground, one of whose buildings was a railway carriage destined for Argentine Railways but sunk on the way and salvaged, Hammond took 134 off Lancashire. The crowd at Ashley Down saw him make an undefeated half-century and then a century. Down in Somerset, below the Quantock Hills and the spires and towers of Taunton, came another hundred. The men of Kent and the Kentish men came to Gravesend, where the home team included the two great England wicket-keepers of the middle years of the century, Ames and T. G. Evans. Evans caught Hammond in the second innings but not before he had made 63, and earlier 80.

So the summer continued. Every crowd which came to watch

Gloucestershire play, with the solitary exception of those at Brentwood, saw at least a Hammond half-century. 'Headquarters' at Bristol was the scene of two double-centuries. Although he played less than half as many innings as any other Gloucestershire batsman, his aggregate was nearly the highest and his average of over 100 was three times that of his nearest rival. That first post-war season for Gloucestershire had been business as usual. Only in the Test series against India did he accomplish less, much less. He was top of the first-class averages at 84.90, well ahead of the leading younger generation of cricketers, which lay far behind with averages in the forties.

Yet those who saw him that summer had a feeling it might be their last chance. Parents and fond relatives took their children so that they might be able to relate the experience. Michael May and his brother were 'taken by the vicar to Southampton, where we lay on the roof of the car watching county cricket for the first time, seeing Hammond make fifty and realising that something very special was happening.' A fifteen-year-old went with his father on August Bank Holiday and saw a double-century. 'Now,' his father said to him, 'you have seen everything.' Patrick Campbell spread the word in an article in *Picture Post*: 'He talks of retiring after Australia. See him while you can. The chances are there'll never be anyone quite like him again, and your grandsons will feel you have let them down if you didn't see Hammond on their behalf.'

For him not to lead England in Australia was unthinkable. 'Was there another man who could have been a sensible alternative?' rhetorically asked *Picture Post*. The choice was logical and in-disputable. He was the reigning England leader and there was no reason to doubt his continuing ability. He had shown, said *Wisden*, 'the batting form that made him almost a terror to bowlers'. But he would be the oldest man ever to captain an England side in Australia, perhaps too old to sustain a long tour with the burden of leadership. In a sense everyone was six years too old. The war had clipped those years off every cricketer. Those in their early twenties had not had the experience of more than a single season of first-class cricket. Evans, the wicket-keeper, at 26 would be the youngest tourist. Hammond had tried hard to persuade his old friend Ames to make a fourth tour of Australia as wicket-keeper batsman, but Ames was adamant that his wicket-keeping days were over.

Hammond himself wanted to lead England in Australia. It would crown a great career. It was not age nor advancing fibrositis which made him hesitate. His concern was for Sybil Ness-Harvey, who had come to England. Eight months was a long time for her to be on her own in a country where she knew scarcely anyone. He arranged for her to stay with his mother. It was not the best of plans but it had to serve. Dorothy's lawyers had meanwhile informed him that divorce proceedings would be undertaken. A few days later he boarded the *Stirling Castle*. He had to put his domestic affairs behind him.

The conditions of austerity Britain were not entirely forgotten on board a ship bearing to their new homes wartime brides and fiancées of Australian servicemen. Only Hammond himself enjoyed really comfortable quarters and players recalled invitations to his cabin suite for soft drinks, the vessel being a 'dry' ship. What was not the least reminiscent of wartime was the food. Menus which gourmets on desert islands dreamed of were set before those who had got used to spam, snoek and reconstituted egg. Tell-tale waistlines crept round fast bowlers. Both Alec Bedser and Voce were borne along to the scales of the ship's butcher. Deck games did something to reduce the damage. Hammond was better than the younger men at deck-tennis and quoits. Less energetically, he played chess with Hardstaff.

The captain tried to give the newcomers some idea of what they would meet in Australia without, as he put it, unduly 'lecturing them'. He let his own philosophy towards the tour be known. He saw its importance in goodwill terms. It may be that a certain mellowness had crept into his own outlook and that to him, cricket was not the stern, death or glory contest which it had once been. Such an attitude, whether right or wrong, was to prove scarcely determined enough against the oldest opponents of all led by a shrewd, ruthless, talented, ambitious skipper in Bradman.

When the team landed in Australia, Hammond was careful to say little beyond indicating the importance of the 'goodwill mission' to which politicians and cricket administrators attached so much weight. Indeed, he may be criticised for saying too little. E. W. Swanton believed he upset an important Sydney journalist, Jim Mathers, who had boarded the ship at Fremantle, by giving him a 'frosty greeting'. But the press as a whole were enthusiastic to set the scene for the series, and gave a great deal of extremely flattering publicity to MCC. The virtues of the bowlers were extolled to the extent that Bradman – with nothing to add to his reputation but everything to lose – hesitated before confirming that he would be available to captain the side.

Bradman's eventual acceptance of the captaincy heralded his own attitude of 'no quarter given or expected'. He remembered the bodyline series of 1932–33 and England's accumulation of over 900 in 1938. If Hammond's men were not up to the standard of the Australian cricketers, then it was too bad. As the Australian journalist Clif Cary put it, 'Hammond and Bradman had completely divergent views on the meaning of cricket goodwill.'

But Hammond held to the conviction that he was leading a team of men who had come through the war and who had lost some of their Test colleagues in the process. He promised the players 'the happiest six months of their lives' and many of them have subsequently testified to their enjoyment of that tour. The captain's 'laissez-faire' attitude may invite criticism but he cannot be accused of being a spoil-sport.

The opening weeks of the tour were deceptively calm. The up-country matches gave players the practice they needed. Hammond himself retired at 131 in the game against Northam. He followed this with 208 in the opening first-class match against Western Australia. It was his thirty-fifth double-century and after passing 200 he could still run a fast single between the wickets. He had batted, said *The Times*, in 'his most masterful manner, all bowlers alike to him'. As memorable for many was his gesture in sitting among blind ex-servicemen during the game and giving them a ball-by-ball commentary on events.

Those who knew him best breathed a sigh of relief. The skipper was fit, in form and at peace with himself. Then a telephone rang in his Perth hotel. Overseas calls in those pre-STD days were beset with crackles. The agitated voice of Sybil came through. She and his mother could not get on. She would be on her own. Yes, she would be all right but . . . . The 'pips' went and Hammond's serenity vanished. Rupert Howard, the manager, knew. Others were left to guess. The emptiness of the Nullabor Plain across which the train to Adelaide bore him became the symbol of his own isolation.

At home the divorce took its course. The reports of his name in a list of undefended petitions to be heard at Leeds Assizes and the subsequent decree nisi were all relayed in the Australian press. Sir Leonard Hutton believed that Hammond 'found the comments of the press most hurtful'.

17. Hammond on his appointment as England captain in 1938. (*Illustrated London News*)

18. Hammond auctions one of his own bats in aid of Reg Sinfield's benefit in 1938, while the beneficiary watches anxiously. (*Gloucestershire Newspapers Ltd*)

19 & 20. The second Test at Lord's in 1938. Batting during his innings of 240 (above – *Illustrated London News*) and being presented by Stanley Baldwin to King George VI (below).

21. Dining with Sybil Ness-Harvey in Durban in 1938 at a function to meet Lord Nuffield. They were to marry after the war. (*Durban Sunday Tribune*)

22. Less than a year later he was commissioned as a pilot officer in the RAF. (*Fox Photos*)

23. Batting against India at Lord's in 1946.
(*Sport and General*)

24. The MCC tour to Australia, 1946–47.
Back row: Jas. Langridge, D. C. S. Compton,
T. G. Evans, L. Hutton. Middle row:
D. V. P. Wright, C. Washbrook, J. T. Ikin,
A. V. Bedser, R. Pollard, T. P. B. Smith, R.
Howard (manager). Front row: W. Voce,
P. A. Gibb, N. W. D. Yardley, W. R.
Hammond, W. J. Edrich, L. Fishlock, J.
Hardstaff.

25. The agony of failure: Hammond caught by Ernie Toshack off Colin McCool in the second Test in 1946–47. (*Illustrated London News*)

26. The joy of parenthood: Hammond with his son, Roger, in 1949.

27. Hammond being presented with his portrait in 1950. On the right the Duke of Beaufort, on Hammond's left, Sir Pelham Warner. (*Bristol Evening News*)

28. Hammond's last game for Gloucestershire. Batting with Arthur Milton in 1951 against Somerset.

29. Hammond's last match near Durban in 1964. On his right, Denis Compton. Far right, D. B. Carr. Head bowed in back row, John Woodcock, later the editor of *Wisden*.

30. The University of Natal XI, 1960–61. Dr Horwood second from left, Hammond second from right. (*Owen Horwood*)

31. The Hammond Oval at the University of Natal in Durban which Hammond did so much to create. (*Gavin Maasdorp*)

32. The last picture of Hammond, taken in his office in the University of Natal in 1964. Compare it with picture 17 nearly thirty years earlier. (*Bruce Vester*)

The team played the eastern States in turn. South Australia were lucky not to be beaten by an innings, Victoria were vanquished, rain interfered against New South Wales and the Queensland game was drawn. Hammond had made a fifty in one game and some speeches which, one reporter noticed, 'had neatness and wit'. He constantly asserted how good for the game was the prospect of Bradman being available. He was putting a brave face on circumstances. With one first-class win behind them the side came to the first Test. Of that first Test played between England and Australia since the war three things need to be said and they relate to Bradman, the Ashes and Hammond respectively.

Bradman, whose hesitancy about returning to international cricket had been well-publicised, was equally hesitant in perform-ance in the opening overs of the game. Coming to the wicket to a tumultuous reception when the total was 9, he was markedly ill at ease and came near to being dismissed on several occasions. When he had made 28, J. T. Ikin at first slip appealed for a catch which the umpire disallowed. The catch came shoulder-high, so there was no question of the ball having hit the ground. Ikin showed his delight rather than roared his appeal. Bradman did not move and an appeal became necessary. A belated request to the umpire brought a rejection. Clif Cary thought it was the worst umpiring blunder he could recall in any grade of cricket. Con-versely, the English journalist, Bruce Harris, from his distant seat 'thought the ball "came off the deck"'. It was fair for Bradman to stand his ground and, as Fingleton remarked, there was never the slightest reason to doubt his sportsmanship.

Hammond kept an impassive face, contenting himself at the end of an over with a mumbled 'What a way to start a series.' To Ikin he commented, 'Well done, Johnnie.' But his reflections were on the standard of umpiring rather than the integrity of Bradman. He was later to say, 'Cricket is full of "ifs" – our job was to get on with the game.' But bad umpiring, in a pre-video-recording age, remained the spectre at the feast for the remainder of the series. Bradman's 'escape' proved the turning-point of his own performance. He himself testified to Hammond's dignity over the whole incident, quoting him as saying at the end of the match, 'I thought it was a catch but I may have been wrong.' The Don's score of 187 led to his decision to continue in Test cricket. At the end of the series his average was 97.14. He then came to England in 1948 to lead a victorious and undefeated side and his great career culminated in the accolade of knighthood. It is not unhistorical to attribute all these events to the disputed 'catch'.

Bradman's long innings at Brisbane affected the destiny of the Ashes. Australia made 645, their highest ever score against England, and dismissed England twice to win by an innings and 332 runs. Figures conceal the fact that England were forced to bat on successive days following two tremendous overnight thunder-storms. Of England's performance on a wicket variously described by the press as 'evil', 'of almost incredible badness', 'utterly un-playable', the critics were full of praise. In the press box Grimmett, whose fingers must have itched to bowl in such conditions, spoke of a 'wonderful mastery of wet wicket play'. Nevertheless, the length of Bradman's innings had prolonged the Australian one as a whole and led to England's two innings when the weather turned. That fact dictated the pattern of the series. England, recognisably the weaker side, had had the worst of the luck.

There remains something to be said on Hammond. He began with an outstanding catch in the third over to dismiss A. R. Morris and bring Bradman in. He batted in England's two innings for the modest totals of 32 and 23. But the figures give the lie and his batting in the conditions was hailed as outstanding. There were 16 runs in one over off E. R. H. Toshack which scoffed at the seven men the bowler had placed round the wicket. Fingleton wrote, 'If I had never seen Hammond play some of the liveliest innings in all cricket creation, I would remember him always for the two classical innings he played on the Brisbane "glue pot". In such circumstances the scoresheet is a fraud and a hum-bug.' Of his own batting Hammond, in his books of reminiscence, modestly had nothing to say. In his personal performance he had given no reason for anyone to doubt his continued mastery. Indeed, the uncertainty with which Bradman had batted at the start had hinted at the Australian skipper rather than the English one declining in skill. The gods laughed at the conclusions of pressmen and spectators as they plotted their own course for Hammond's batting future.

The game had ended at ten minutes to five. Soon Hammond set off in his car to drive to Sydney. Both Washbrook and Hutton recalled one of the strangest car journeys of their lives. Hammond drove all the way, fast, yet safely. His only utterances were a request to have his cigarette lit or for one of his two companions to knock up a petrol station attendant – well into the night when petrol was not normally available after six o'clock. The journey of some 900 miles was undertaken with barely a stop. Hammond was alone with his thoughts.

Towards the end of the third day of the second Test at Sydney, Australia began to pull ahead. S. G. Barnes and Bradman had been together for nearly 100 and the first innings lead had been secured. Those back in a savagely cold British winter who tuned in their wirelesses to a crackly reception in the cold and darkness of early morning felt mildly uneasy. Bradman, not out for 52, signalled a threat. It was a bad way to start a Monday morning, muttered the commuters as they made their way to work.

There was no comfort 24 hours later. It was still bitterly cold in Britain, and Barnes and Bradman were still there in brilliant sunshine in Australia. Wirelesses were switched off as people left to catch trains and buses. Only those able to enjoy a late breakfast at home were consoled with the wickets of both of them just before play ended. They had put on 405 for the fifth wicket. Each had made 234 and Australia had, in two matches running, scored their highest total against England. The defeat which followed was not without honour. England's 371 left them losers by an innings and 33 runs but they had batted attractively. Hutton's 37, by general acclaim, was an innings of grace and skill. Hammond's 37 was full of attack. Edrich's century won the crowd's goodwill. But the old year ended with England two down and three to play and not since 1897–98 had an England side lost two Test matches running by an innings. Knives were being sharpened.

Three minor matches and Christmas came between the second and third Tests. Hammond made a century against the Northern Districts of New South Wales in the large coal-mining centre of Newcastle and was easily the highest scorer for MCC overall. His Christmas Day was spent with friends and he presented his team to the Governor-General, the Duke of Gloucester, at Canberra two days later. The Melbourne Test – the one England had to win to keep the series alive – was a draw. Hammond played a second innings of 26 which had great promise of being more. He was beaten by the pace of Ray Lindwall in poor light. 'Majestic strokes flashed the ball through the covers like the Hammond of old,' commented McCabe in the Melbourne *Age*.

The press were less kind to him over his captaincy. He was criticised for allowing the Australian tail-enders to score 'the best part of 200 runs' on the off-side through wide-open gaps while retaining three unnecessary slips and a deep gully. Ringside observers also felt that there was a lack of contact between the captain and his bowlers. 'He sailed like a schooner from slip to slip anchorage with hardly a consultation,' wrote Fingleton. To one of the bowlers, 'He seemed to use us by formula. We were changed around after a prescribed interval.' It was a hard judgement not entirely borne out by the evidence of the detailed daily press reports. By contrast, a spectator walking into the ground ignorant of the game and its personalities would have identified Bradman as captain of a fielding side within moments. Conductors lead their orchestras in different ways. The unobtrusive gesture can bring in the second violins at just the right moment. Hammond was by nature undemonstrative; flamboyant gestures would have been foreign to him.

The third Test, as the other two, had been plagued by controversial umpiring decisions. The Melbourne *Sporting Globe* commented that 'they wrecked the whole atmosphere'. England got the worse of the rub in this and it was much to Hammond's credit that he accepted the disappointments with dignity.

His decision not to accompany the team to Tasmania brought criticism from the *Sunday Express* which printed a cabled report stating, 'Many think that Hammond should not be having a rest in Melbourne while the team is in Tasmania.' The report received wide coverage on all Australian radio networks and led to the manager, Major Howard, defending the captain's 'need of a rest'.

Hammond had been stoically and typically silent about the ill-health which he had suffered during the tour, and he remained so as long as he could. The rest was beneficial and he set about the South Australian bowling three weeks later with an innings of 188. Out of an MCC total of 577, Hammond shared in a sixth-wicket partnership of 243 with James Langridge. In sweltering heat, the two oldest tourists batted in the grand manner. The Adelaide crowd, had they but known it, were witnessing an historic event. Never again would Hammond make a century in first-class cricket. It was his hundred and sixty-seventh and his last. Only Hendren and Hobbs eclipsed him. Those three, with C. P. Mead, seem likely to remain the only men in first-class cricket to score over 150 centuries.

The match provided another landmark for Hammond: he became the seventh man to score 50,000 runs in first-class cricket, joining the three other men with 150 centuries, Woolley, Grace and Sutcliffe. Immediately afterwards there was another 'last'. Hammond took the field for the fourth Test match. He would never again appear in a first-class match in Australia. His final gesture was to set Australia a target to chase; to make something of a match in which both sides had scored over 450 in their first innings; to express his belief that that post-war tour was more a Renaissance for the game than another campaign in a Hundred Years' War. But England faced a dour and combative Australia: Bradmen's men did not take up the challenge of winning at the risk of losing.

So Hammond walked from the stage of Anglo-Australian cricket with 40 runs in his last game and a slip catch. Of his very last innings, *The Times* remarked that he played 'with confidence and serenity'. He was praised for the declaration he had made. He had kept on taking the fight to the Australians. And so, as in Carlyle's judgement on Danton, he had passed by, this man of valour. He would live for some generations in the memory of men. He had been worth showing to the people.

The gold-diggers of Ballarat had the last Australian look at Hammond. He fielded until lunch, when illness forced him to quit. Five weeks of cricket remained in Australia: five weeks in which the captain, crippled by fibrositis, took no part. The role of non-playing captain was not easy, nor was paying farewell visits to other Australian state capitals on whose fields he had been expected to make a final appearance. He walked to the middle with N. W. D. Yardley to inspect the wicket at Sydney for the fifth Test and then handed the captaincy to the first Yorkshireman to lead an English side in Australia. Up to the last minute he had hoped to play but twenty-four hours earlier he could barely move without pain. England lost a tight game by five wickets. Had Hammond been at slip, Bradman might have gone for two and the game been won. From the dressing room Hammond gave much good advice. There was an ironic determination about his absentee leadership which had been missing in some of the earlier games. The absence of having to perform seemed to sharpen his critical judgement.

The long tour concluded with a visit to New Zealand. To everyone's delight he was able to play and so take part in his eighty-fifth and last Test match. The New Zealand cricketers and crowd, conscious of the moment, cheered him all the way to the wicket. Hammond had always loved New Zealand. He smiled his appreciation and set out to merit their applause. Ikin recalled the occasion:

England were not in a strong position when I joined Hammond. In the first few overs I found difficulty in facing the left-arm spin of Burtt. Hammond came down the wicket and said, 'I'll take him, Johnnie, don't worry.' For over after over, Hammond ensured that he himself faced Burtt while I gained confidence.

Ikin admitted that to cricketers of his generation Hammond was a hero. 'The sense of hero-worship never left me.' He remembered courtesies on the outward-bound trip to Australia, a welcome in Hammond's cabin-suite, the words of sympathy when the famous 'catch' was disallowed. That last partnership left a pleasant taste. The match and the tour ended in rain. As Hammond walked off the field so he walked out of Ikin's ken. The two men never met again.

Hammond had made 781 runs during the tour for an average of 41.10. He had scored two centuries and a further two in minor matches. Only in the Tests had his record been disappointing. That great supporter of the game, Sir Robert Menzies, Lord's Taverner and prime minister of Australia, observed during the fourth Test that it was 'a part of the eternal justice of things that Walter Hammond should play at least one great innings every Test series'. It was not to be, yet in the view of some of the critics it might well have happened. 'Several times during those small innings the old touch seemed to be coming back when he was out,' wrote Bruce Harris of the *Evening Standard*. He was often genuinely unlucky, as E. W. Swanton observed: 'His very last stroke in Australia, a swinging leg-hit, looked worth four runs but was marvellously caught by Lindwall 20 yards from the bat.' The point may be made that Bradman enjoyed the breaks and Hammond did not. It was no true reflection of their abilities at that stage in their careers that 76 runs separated them in their batting averages for these Tests. So much for Hammond the batsman. Hammond the bowler does not come into the reckoning – 24 balls were all he dared attempt.

What of Hammond the captain? At the outset of the tour Swanton had expressed his doubts about Hammond's suitability as captain of a touring side despite the praise he had given him in South Africa. He doubted whether the word of encouragement would be given when it was needed and he felt that Hammond's natural talents made it difficult for him to understand 'the problems faced by less gifted mortals'.

To some extent, Swanton was proved right. Hammond with his personal problems complicated by ill-health and a failure to score heavily in the Tests became the remote figure which

critics throughout his career were all too ready to label him anyway. Edrich, with great reluctance, for he liked the man and was
his friend, found him 'edgy, retiring and irritable'. Edrich also
believed that Hammond's coolness to Bradman after the first Test
was carried too far. Not only did Hammond never have a meal with
Bradman, he frowned on other England players who did. He
behaved with icy correctness over many months when a brief but
fiery row might have been better for all concerned. Yet it was not
just the Ikin 'catch'. Hammond and Bradman differed on the
nature of the contest and it may be that Bradman was right. The
'no-holds-barred' school of thought will always have its adherents
from the village game upwards, and the paying public watching
the fight for the Ashes were entitled to expect no quarter given.

As the disappointments came, so Hammond became the butt of
some Australian critics. He began the tour well in the view of
several of his fellow-players. He did not stand on ceremony and he
won their confidence. But if a week is a long time in politics, six
months is a long time in cricket. As time went by, Hammond
seemed to lose the dynamism to lead, the determination to win,
the self-confidence to prosper. Even his great admirer, Warner,
felt he just 'let the game go on' in the third Test as two tail-
enders added over 150 runs in an hour. Clif Cary, though often
sympathetic to Hammond, took a hard line on his captaincy: 'It
lacked applied intelligence, thought and inspiration.'

Some of his major batsmen felt also that they were getting the
wrong advice about how to play the Australian slow bowlers. The
instinct of Compton, for example, was to go out to the ball. Hammond, able to play slow bowlers from within the crease himself
(and, indeed, he had done so in his successful tour of 1928–29),
advised Compton to do the same. Yet with bowlers like C. L. Mc-
Cool and Ian Johnson, going out to meet them was half the battle.

The choice of players for the Tests also brought some comment.
No touring captain makes a selection autocratically – although
some, such as Jardine, have come near to doing so – but Hammond
and his fellow-selectors were slow in spotting the wicket-keeping
talents of Evans. Thus Gibb had plenty of matches before the first
Test in which his performance both in batting (where there were
high expectations of him) and wicket-keeping was indifferent.
Only in the second Test did Evans get his chance to prove that
he would be the outstanding English wicket-keeper of the next
15 years.

There were critics Hammond could have done without – notably, the Yorkshire captain, A. B. Sellers, who was in Australia as a journalist. Sellers himself may be criticised on two counts. As a selector, he had helped to pick Hammond and it was scarcely his business later to stab him in the back. Secondly, he attacked Hammond very early in the tour, before the Brisbane Test, when the grounds were slight. Hammond, to his great credit, never made a word of complaint about Sellers' reporting and was seen chatting to him from time to time.

Let us take one final area of criticism and then have done. Hammond chose to drive round Australia for most of the tour rather than go by train. He and his manager usually went together. Of course the captain should have been with the team more than he was, but, as one of them said, 'We were mostly ex-servicemen. It was nice not to have the "CO" breathing down our necks.' Hammond's own defence was this: 'Modern Test touring practice is far more likely to develop too much discipline than too little. The team was none the worse for a little freedom.'

In fact, the players from that tour were ready to speak up in Hammond's defence to a surprising extent. They were loyal, not prepared to hear a word against him, concerned for him in his batting failures, aware of his domestic crisis. Taking up the 'ex-service' theme, another said, 'It was to his credit that he chose not to inhibit our sense of liberty by his authoritarian presence.'

Both Ikin and Washbrook admired his restraint over the umpiring issues which arose throughout the tour. Had he chosen, he could have made a dramatic tirade against the standard of umpiring. Instead, he protested with the utmost reluctance, privately and discreetly to the Australian Board of Control, and with the insistence that it was standards and not partiality which concerned him. After the tour, he wrote, 'The umpiring was quite impartial in intent; the games were good and keen in every way; to exaggerate a few human errors is to lose a sense of proportion.' It was a diplomatic remark which did him credit. The players also believed their skipper did what was asked of him as a speaker, especially to Australian audiences all too ready to be on the defensive against Jardinian-style speeches. Social duties did not come easily. He carried them out much more than adequately if scarcely triumphantly.

At the end of the tour he gave a broadcast on Australian radio which was extremely well-received. Alan McGilvray told me how anxious and diffident Hammond was before it, insisting that McGilvray should 'vet' what he was going to say. Hammond was not the supremely confident man which his great performances on the field made him appear. When the performances were less than great or when he was away from the field entirely he was unsure of himself: more ready for support than many would have dreamed. Hardstaff spotted this: 'There was a worried look on his face when he failed. I knew him well, played chess with him. I thought it a big mistake to make him captain: it was more than he could take.' Clif Cary, from an Australian angle, made this considered judgement:

> On the credit side of Hammond's visit to Australia was the grand job he did in the interests of the game. He played it as only a thorough sportsman could. He accepted the grimness of certain opponents without so much as an 'off the record' protest; he stood up to heavy rollers and unshaven wickets without demur, and while on tour kept secret the fact that he was not satisfied with umpires, wickets or the over-bowling of bumpers.
>
> Hammond did not think of himself. He displayed tact and diplomacy in the interests of cricket, and wherever they went his colleagues were welcomed and liked. Individually, and collectively, the team was perhaps the most popular sporting combination ever to come from England, and it was skipper Hammond who helped win for them this off-the-field friendship which, to a great extent, compensated for their on-the-field failures.

The press also showed their sympathy for him in that last Test at Sydney. Bradman was cheered all the way to the pavilion by a tumultuous crowd – yet he indicated that he had not retired, and it was a hero's farewell for a hero who had five more Test centuries yet to make. Hammond sat disconsolate in the pavilion while the Sydney crowd, who had witnessed some of his greatest deeds, would have been generous in their acclamation had he been able to take the field to receive it. If he had stayed in Test cricket too long, he had done it for the best of motives, to help the post-war game recover. There was nothing in it for him and he knew it.

The tribute of Norman Preston in *Wisden* should not go un-noticed. He assessed the problems Hammond faced in 1946–47 and he rated highly his handling of them: 'No England captain could have had under him a more loyal set of men. All of them would have done anything for him. They appreciated his vast experience of Australia and did their best to order their play in the way he wished.'

That Hammond was a man in pain, both physical and mental, needs to be re-affirmed. Fibrositis finally had its way, affecting his back and making movement difficult. Washbrook vividly recollected Hammond pouring aspirin down himself in the dressing-room at Adelaide to alleviate the pain. Yet he struck 188 runs there. There were only one or two men who were intimate enough with him to know that for Hammond personal happiness at last lay within his grasp. The manager was his travelling colleague and what they said to each other the biographer can only guess at.

In going to Australia he had endeavoured to serve the cause of English cricket. He went at the behest of the cricketing authorities who saw him as the natural person to lead the first overseas tour. Some of those close to him had tried hard to persuade him not to go, among them F. O. Wills, the Gloucestershire chairman, who believed that the personal strain which Hammond was undergoing was too great for him to assume the extra burden of captaincy. 'He was foolish to accept in the circumstances,' was the view of Wills's son, G. H. Wills, who also knew Hammond at the time.

So, some twelve thousand miles from home and amid the glare of publicity and the scars of defeat, Wally Hammond played his cricket and suffered his personal agony. The nearest he got to talking about it in print came when he wrote about the problem of playing the game with one's mind elsewhere, 'going down the pitch to a bowler and thinking painfully of something else altogether.' In defeat he was generous in tribute to his opponents: 'I revelled in the sight of their dauntless, picturesque, happy youth, giving to the game we love something we older players could no longer offer it.'

With these memories of an Australia he had loved over 20 years from his first visit, 'callow, eager, unfledged', to his last, he arrived back in England on 9 April 1947. On 10 April he married Sybil Ness-Harvey in London and they had a reception in the Park Lane Hotel. Both these events were duly recorded in the press.

On 11 April a personal letter went from the president of MCC, General Sir Ronald Adam, to the Director-General of the BBC, Sir William Haley, asking if Hammond might do a broadcast at peak listening time to dispel the belief in England that the tour had been a failure in social terms as much as in cricketing ones. 'It was a goodwill mission and was very successful as such. The team were astonished when they got home to hear that there were any doubts on the subject or that there were any doubts in Australia.' Adam went on to say how much the players had been conscious of the gifts to Britain of clothing and of food parcels and of the personal kindnesses they themselves had received.

Haley at once set events in motion and within ten days Hammond was contracted to make a 15-minute broadcast after the nine o'clock news. The script would also be relayed at a later date to the Pacific Service for Australian and New Zealand listeners. Hammond lunched with the talks producer when he had written his piece. The Secretary of MCC, Colonel Rait Kerr, was sent a copy 24 hours in advance with instructions to phone any comments or criticisms to the BBC in time for changes to be made. On 6 May 1947 Hammond gave his broadcast:

> We didn't succeed in bringing home the Ashes but in every other way the tour was a success. We were received with the greatest hospitality and kindness. It was quite clear to me that people in Australia and New Zealand did appreciate the fact that we had sent a team at all. With all humility we can claim that our visit has done something to cement the relationship between this country and Australia and New Zealand. As a goodwill tour it was a complete success.

He repeated the accepted reasons for defeat: the failure of medium-pace bowlers to get life from the wickets, the lack of a bowler of real pace and the inability of proven batsmen (including himself) to score a lot of runs. He was generous in his tribute to the Australians and considerate towards the umpires whose efforts and impartiality he never doubted but whose standards fell below Test match expectations. There was, he concluded, 'no reason to be despondent about our cricket', and 'no nicer or happier side ever travelled.'

This public statement was heard both at home and in the Antipodes. Hammond had discharged his final duty as an England captain. He had not felt it his business to comment on his own personal affairs nor, in particular, to defend charges of his remoteness as a captain.

The need for urgent correspondence at high level between the MCC president and the BBC Director-General seems, at this distance of time, somewhat unnecessary. But Adam was far too busy a man to pursue an unnecessary cause. He had just become Director-General of the British Council and he regarded good relations within the Commonwealth as of major importance. And we need to remind ourselves that the bodyline controversy was still a recent memory. No-one wanted anything other than harmony to prevail between England and Australia either on the cricket field or off it. England in 1947 still needed those food parcels. Everyone wanted to be reassured that the cricketers had been ambassadors for austerity Britain.

That broadcast gave the listening public in Britain a chance to hear Hammond's voice. He had spoken on the BBC in 1927 and he had used a loud-hailer in his pre-war recruiting. For the first time, millions heard him speak. His performance was impressive. Every syllable and consonant was clearly enunciated. His delivery varied in pace with a slow, deliberate emphasis on the things he thought important. The voice was accentless, deep and authoritative. From the opening sentence, it commanded attention. The listener would have switched off his set reluctantly. Some months later he gave another broadcast. The occasion was the Week's Good Cause and he appealed on behalf of the Birmingham ENT Hospital. The debt which he felt he owed to good nursing and his personal liking for children both found expression. He began by taking his listeners back to 1926, 'a year of short skirts, the General Strike and the Australians in England'. For him it was the year he lay at the point of death. He recalled vividly the care and devotion of those who had tended him all that summer and he indicated that half the patients of the hospital for which he was appealing were children. 'Children are so pitiful when they are hurt and they trust grown-ups to take that hurt away.' His appeal brought in over £500 and was one of the most successful regional appeals of the year.

Soon he himself was a family man with a son of his own. He and Sybil had set up home at Thrupp House in Gloucestershire where Roger was born in 1948. There they were to be very happy for eighteen months, a halcyon period.

Thrupp House, on the outskirts of Stroud, commands views from every window – Stroud itself, rising hillsides, a deep valley, clusters of small houses and farmsteads, rolling landscape, the railway to London and the derelict Thames–Severn canal. The house was built by a Victorian businessman of substance whose profits in the growing prosperity of Bristol allowed him to establish a place of minor distinction for his family. A coat-of-arms is set above the colonnade which creates a gracious entrance. Floral capitals adorn each column. Cotswold stone gives antiquity to the nineteenth-century mock-castellated frontage. A large Victorian family with a retinue of servants had lived here. Spacious rooms had housed heavy mahogany furniture, wide staircases had borne buckets of coal and jugs of hot water, gardens were a setting for tennis or tea. The fabric of life in this Gloucestershire haven seemed to have an unending pattern. Victorian optimism lingered until 1914.

Two world wars later found Walter Hammond taking his new bride to Thrupp House and there, with the Gracies and the Andersons as fellow-tenants, creating for himself a new life. The rent was £80 a year and for that they had a top-floor flat with three fine rooms and a hall. Sybil responded with pleasure to the adulation which her husband still commanded. Soon her husband was confessing to Joyce Gracie that he was happier than he had ever been before in his life.

To a cricket enthusiast such as Joyce Gracie it was, of course, a thrill having a famous cricketer as a neighbour. 'The famous cricketer,' she corrected herself. 'I had seen him in the 1920s and 1930s. He was wonderful to watch. To see him play was out of this world.' She paused and remembered watching Grace and Jessop as a young girl. 'I was brought up on them but Hammond was still the greatest of them all.'

So did she judge, this sprightly old Victorian lady, upon a man's world. 'I was thrilled to have him as a neighbour but I didn't pester him by talking cricket.' But talk they did – about Hammond's childhood, the sadder side of his first marriage, his relationship with his mother. There were outings in which the Gracies went with the younger couple. A day at Blenheim Palace was 'great fun. People recognised him – he didn't mind that! He signed autographs and Sybil enjoyed seeing people admire him. He enjoyed the majesty of that great house and then a simple tea.'

One evening the Gracies gave a party. Joyce issued one instruction in advance: no-one was to talk about cricket. People chatted and 'we played silly games.' The time came to leave and Hammond remarked, 'I haven't enjoyed an evening so much for years.' 'He let his hair down, didn't mind playing the fool, helped everyone to have a grand time.' One day he drove Joyce and her husband to Leamington. She asked if his Jaguar could do a hundred. He responded and, for a brief spell, gave her the thrill of seeing the speedometer reach the figures which, in cricketing terms, had so often been his own goal. When Roger was born it was Joyce who found an old Victorian dress of her own childhood for a long christening robe. 'He was a devoted father and he told me he was thrilled to be a parent.'

Noël Anderson would come home for weekends from nursing at St Thomas's in London to stay with her parents in the other flat. She, too, saw in Hammond a happiness and pleasantness of manner which she took for granted. The complexity of his character, and the moroseness with which many associated him, were unknown to her. 'He was a good companion, for example, driving up to London one evening.' There was a dance in Gloucestershire organised by the indefatigable Joyce Gracie. The Hammonds and Andersons went and there Noël Anderson met Henry Witchell, who had been a contemporary of Hammond's in the Cirencester School XI, and whom she later married. Witchell had gone on to play for Wiltshire and topped the Minor Counties batting averages in 1934. So another cricketing influence joined the small circle at Thrupp House. Noël's father, Robert, played golf with Wally.

Meanwhile Hammond continued his business life with Marsham Tyres, travelling up to London, and he was under contract to write for the London *Star* on the 1948 Test series against Australia. In one article he made a strong plea for wickets which gave bowlers a chance. He was also engaged in writing the four books on cricket which Stanley Paul published between 1947 and 1951. Frank Stuart was employed as the ghost-writer.

Stuart's methods were to make his 'author' work hard. Hammond had to draft his ideas on paper. Sybil recalled many a winter evening when he scribbled away. Literacy did not come easily to him and the few letters available to his biographer confirm this. But ideas and sentiments were expressed on which Stuart could build. Stuart would interview Hammond and ask for further elucidation on what he had drafted. The result was a set of books which throw considerable light on Hammond's reaction to the events of his professional career. They confirm the modesty to which many have testified. They show a concern for the young cricketer which was all too often lacking in his playing career: he found it difficult to appreciate that others could not match his own abilities, but a more generous recognition of this comes out in his books. The coaching he was reluctant to give found expression in *Cricketers' School*, published in 1950.

Cricket My Destiny and *Cricket My World* are largely biographical while *Cricket's Secret History* is a somewhat discursive book which touches on the future of the game. The books as a whole give away very little about the man himself.

A chance to recall old memories and his hundredth hundred came in a BBC invitation to participate in 'Scrapbook for 1935'. Another invitation to take part in a programme had to be declined because he was abroad in South Africa on his firm's business. The BBC files reveal that his few contributions were valued and that there might have been a future for him as a regular broadcaster on cricket.

In 1949 the Hammond family moved to Esher in Surrey, where he played some cricket for the local club, and a year later they moved again to the village of Cuffley in Hertfordshire. Cuffley recruited Hammond for a match. 'Our usual "gate" swelled from 20 to 100. He made about 60 for us, a most friendly person,' remembered one player.

During 1950 and 1951 three events marked the effective end of his association with the English first-class game. In March 1950, at the annual Gloucestershire dinner, he was presented with his portrait, painted by Edward Halliday, RBA. In his tribute, Sir Pelham Warner said:

> I come here tonight to praise not to bury Walter Hammond because his splendid deeds on the cricket field can never be buried. He is one of the immortals. If cricket lasts a thousand years – as it undoubtedly will – Hammond's name will always have a tremendous place in the history of cricket.

Other speeches came from the Duke of Beaufort, the county president; Colonel Rait Kerr, the MCC secretary; and Beverley Lyon, the former captain. In the eulogies necessarily associated with such occasions, two themes stood out – the greatness of Hammond as a player and his sportsmanship.

In his reply Hammond, almost overcome with emotion, paid tribute to all those players and officials he had known at Bristol.

> I have had, I suppose, my fair share of proud and exciting moments, but this evening will always remain in my memory as one of the proudest and most moving events of my life. My association with the Gloucestershire club has been long and extremely happy.
> I feel it should really be I who should give something to the club

in appreciation of the happy years I have spent with it. I only hope that the solution that I have found will be accepted in the spirit in which it is offered.

The 'solution' was to present the club with a copy of the portrait undertaken by the same artist. It is the picture represented on the jacket of this book.

The second event may be traced in that obscure part of *Wisden* known as Other Matches. At Dublin in September 1950, Hammond played for MCC against Ireland. *Wisden* stated that 'he showed much of his former punishing powers', while his skipper declared when the former England captain was eight runs short of a century. Hammond had been known to do the same to himself!

Finally, there was one last appearance for Gloucestershire in the August Bank Holiday fixture against Somerset in 1951. A picture shows him striving to make his ground after a sharp call from 23-year-old Arthur Milton, a future England batsman. The Ashley Down ground was packed and they cheered Hammond again and again. Even that normally staid figure, Colonel Henson, the county secretary, could be seen 'leaning out of the window, waving and shouting like a madman'. It was 31 years since a 17-year-old, wearing his Cirencester School cap, had made 7 at Cheltenham. He made another 7 in this game at Bristol and about 50,000 in between.

10
South African Enterprise, 1951–65

'At the age of 58, the old master
had not lost his craft.'
The *Natal Daily News*, 1961

Hammond's letter of resignation dropped into the in-tray of the managing director of Marsham Tyres one autumn day in 1951. Bill Pope was sorry to read it, for he had valued more and more the role played by his sales director, whose decision to leave the firm with which he had been associated since 1937 had been reached for a variety of reasons. Britain, still in the grip of rationing and fuel controls six years after the war, appealed little to his wife, to whom the climate of her native South Africa beckoned. Hammond himself had always enjoyed his visits to South Africa, the last as recent as 1949, but most important was the plan which he and his sales manager, Richard Wilkins, had been discussing.

Wilkins was a man with a first-class head for business and was valued at Marsham as much as Hammond. Two letters of resignation, not just one, had landed on Pope's desk. Wilkins wanted to go out to South Africa primarily because of his wife's health. Thus the two men, colleagues and friends, set out with their families in November 1951 to start their own business in Durban. There were four Hammonds: the parents, Roger, and Carolyn, born in 1950.

Four times Hammond had left England bound for South Africa to play cricket: as a youngster to recuperate, twice as a member of an MCC side and a third time as captain of one. This latest voyage was different for he went as an emigrant. When two weeks later the vessel docked at Cape Town beneath the great slab of Table Mountain, his emotions must have been similar to those of countless settlers since the first British pioneers over a century and a half earlier.

For all emigrants are separatists. Old friends, relations and associations are set aside for a new commitment. Would the commitment prosper? Would a livelihood be established? Such thoughts must have been his as he left the ship, bought a car and drove north to meet his family and the Wilkins as the vessel docked at Durban. He passed Kingsmead on the way to the docks, scene of one of his finest innings in the Timeless Test 12 years earlier, and perhaps he spared himself a memory, shrugged his shoulders and put it behind him. There was fresh work to do.

Wilkins and Hammond set about finding a place to set up their business enterprise. Weeks went by before they found a place for which a capital sum of £10,000 was required. Then things went wrong. They found that their collective resources were far below their needs. Information which should have been exchanged long before they left England had remained undeclared. And so, with a handshake, they went their separate ways. Wilkins would one day become highly successful in South Africa.

From tyres to motor-cars was a short step. News that the great Hammond was job-hunting reached the ears of a Durban businessman, Norman Marshall, who offered him the post of general manager of Denham Motors in West Street which was (and is) the centre of the Durban car trade. To walk down it is to see firm after firm selling new and second-hand cars. End to end, the stock available would stretch some miles out into the Indian Ocean whose waves lap against Durban's shores at the foot of West Street.

The Hammonds bought no. 98, The Fairway in Durban North, a house looking out across that same ocean. Soon afterwards, in 1952, Valerie was born. Their family fortunes prospered in tune with the prosperity in the car industry. 'You did not need to be a salesman to sell a car,' commented a colleague of those days. After two years, the family moved up-market to Knelsby Avenue in Hillcrest. At the same time Wally was elected to the Thursday Golf Club, an exclusive association of a dozen leading businessmen who met once a week for lunch and golf. Hammond's membership was reminiscent of earlier occasions in his life: fame and his ability as a golfer winning him entrée into circles somewhat above his own natural station. Hugh Gormley recalled him 'enjoying the chit-chat, taking part in competitions, being generally sociable'.

Cricket played little part in his life in these years. He turned out in a match soon after taking over Denham Motors but not again for over two years, when he appeared at Kingsmead in October 1955. The game was a charity one, organised by the Round Table. Before a crowd of 5000 he scored 57, including three sixes off the Springbok Ian Smith, declared that he had enjoyed himself immensely and announced next morning that he felt stiff. There-after there were occasional appearances in charity games. He made a rare comment on cricket when he criticised England's batting in the 1958 Brisbane Test against Australia: 'Cricket would be a lot better for a little more of the Norman O'Neill kind of aggression. The tendency in recent years has been for cricketers to play a little guardedly,' he told the London *Evening News* by telephone.

By 1959 the demand for cars had declined. South Africa's 'motor-town' felt the gusts of this recession. Denham Motors faltered and the parent company closed the business down. Hammond was out of a job. Denham Motors was a victim of the economic situation and no blame need be attached to its general manager for its collapse. Yet the point needs to be made that Hammond had been far happier at Marsham than at Denham. The Durban job made more routine day-to-day demands on him, for which he was temperamentally unsuited. Nor did his South African employers get the best out of him. There was no-one who secured the dedication from him that Charles Guyatt and Bill Pope had done. The Marsham days had been his best in business. Ham-mond, at 56, was once again job-hunting. His resources had taken a buffeting. Money put into the firm was lost and a salary, with commission, had ceased. The future was uncertain and the three children were still young.

In the days of Hammond's infancy at Dover, the 1904 South Africans had come to nearby Canterbury to play Kent. Kent had much the best of the game, eventually setting the South Africans 193 to win. Against Colin Blythe their chances were slight, only a last-wicket stand of 60 keeping their hopes alive. That brave but unsuccessful rearguard action was led by Stanley Horwood, whose 34 was second top score in the innings. Horwood was a Western

Province player and captain of Cape Town. Many years later, in 1930, he took his 14-year-old son, Owen, to watch MCC playing a friendly match some miles out of Cape Town. Nearby was some water and the next man in was found to be swimming when expected to bat! A hasty summons brought Wally Hammond back from his swim to the wicket and young Horwood had his first sight of the man with whom he would one day be a close colleague and friend.

Eight years further on found father and son going to Newlands, Cape Town, to watch the 1938–39 England side play South Africa. Stanley Horwood introduced the 22-year-old undergraduate to the England captain. Owen Horwood remembered two things about him on that occasion: his 'imperial presence' and his 'unhurried readiness to make conversation'. The younger Horwood concluded a brilliant university career at Cape Town, went on to captain Cape Town city club for six seasons in First League cricket and quickly established himself as one of the outstanding economists in South Africa. In 1957 he became professor of economics at Natal University. A university set in such a potentially fine campus deserved, he thought, to achieve more in sport. Cricket was at a low ebb and the side did not participate in a league. The professor, newly-elected president of the Athletic Union, was determined to do something about it.

One afternoon Professor Horwood went to watch Hammond in a charity game. He went with a mission. The university had authorised him to look for someone to become its first sports administrator and Horwood believed he had found his man. So Wally Hammond, within a few weeks of the collapse of Denham Motors, was offered the new post at Natal University. His return to sport, and more particularly to cricket, in 1959 began a period of years which was immensely fruitful for him and for the university; the more remarkable in that his achievements remained virtually unknown outside South Africa and only moderately known beyond the borders of Natal. Far from being 'the man who cut the grass', as one well-known cricketer commented to the English press, he proved to be a major influence on the development of South Africa University cricket in the 1960s and on Provincial and Springbok cricket itself.

His appointment, confirmed by the Finance and General Purposes Committee of the University Council, was made in October 1959. £102,000 (a substantial sum from university resources in those days) was allocated to the development of university facilities at both Durban and Pietermaritzburg. The project embraced the construction of tennis and squash courts, a swimming pool, a multi-purpose students' union with facilities for indoor sports and the laying out of a new cricket ground and athletics track. The moving spirit behind all this was Horwood but the execution of it all was placed in Hammond's hands.

The cricket scene, as Hammond first surveyed it, left much to be desired. That the university had not been able to play league cricket could be explained by the poor nets on uneven grass and an inadequate square. Hammond had new nets established and he planned the creation of a field from the sub-tropical bush surrounding the Durban campus. But within a few months fate struck him a cruel blow. He was motoring in February 1960 to Pietermaritzburg, the other part of the university, to do some coaching when he was involved in a crash with a lorry. He had always been a fast driver but the accident was not due to any error on his part. His car rolled over and over and he was left for dead by a police vehicle anxious to get to another accident where a life might be saved. Only the timely intervention of a doctor passing by and seeing the motionless body saved Hammond's own life. He was taken to Grey's Hospital, Pietermaritzburg. Owen Horwood, visiting him the next day, was shocked by what he saw.

Hammond's amazing physical stamina pulled him through. When he returned home in March the tireless devotion of Sybil helped him to recover the use of his limbs. By such simple devices as putting a cup of tea out of reach when he asked for it, she forced him to use his arms. By the middle of the year he was back at work so that the larger part of all he did at the university belonged to the period after the accident.

What pleased his friends most was his re-appearance on the cricket field 18 months after the accident. In November 1961 he turned out for the Hillcrest Moths, a team of ex-servicemen, against the Escombe Moths. The fixture was not among the most distinguished in which he had participated but his own perform-ance, under the circumstances, matched those of his greatest days. The helpless and scarred accident victim of 1960 became the centurion of 1961. He reached his century in 2½ hours. The *Natal Daily News* reported:

Bowlers on an adjacent green left their woods where they lay and passers-by watched with rapt attention. Wally Hammond was in action again, and at the age of 58 the old master had not lost his craft.

He took a reasonably discreet look at the bowling for a while, warmed to the task and then thrashed his way to a century before throwing away his wicket.

The Hammond cover drive, once the joy of cricket the world over, was still there – and with five sixes and 13 fours he treated Escombe to an exciting flashback to the pre-war days of one of the greatest figures the game has known.

Meanwhile he had picked up the threads of his job at the university and the various projects planned in 1959 were completed. The end-product of the cricket one was a fine oval with a brick pavilion, a surround of trees and white fencing, and a wicket which, in the view of many competent cricketers was – and remains – the best in Durban. It was his greatest contribution to Natal University and, in his own modest way, he was a proud man at the official opening ceremony (some years after the ground had been in regular use) in November 1964.

A few weeks before the ceremony, the journalist Marshall Lee, who had been university captain in Hammond's first year, went to see what had been achieved:

There was a poignant moment in the scorers' box from which we looked out over the field, empty but for an Indian groundsman mowing the pitch and a group of colourful women squatting as they weeded. It was a far cry from the Long Room at Lord's and there was, I feel, a flash of nostalgia when I mentioned it, but we soon spoke of something else.

The groundsman was Mari, who was responsible to Hammond for the day-to-day maintenance of the grounds. When I visited the university in 1982 Mari had been long dead but colleagues who had known him bore faithful testimony to his opinion of Hammond: 'He was a good boss.' The beautiful condition of the extensive playing fields was a tribute to the work of the 32 men who worked on them, but their leader, 'Div' de Villiers, was ready to tell me that it all stemmed from Hammond's work 20 years earlier.

The undergraduates of the day, as they passed briefly through the university, saw the amenities develop – each year an improvement on the year before. Perhaps they tended to take that side of Hammond's work for granted. What they assuredly did not take for granted was his role as coach. Their recollections of him are a testimony to what he achieved. Bruce Moor, another past captain, recalled:

> I had been suffering from a run of low scores, despite apparently striking the ball reasonably well at nets. I turned to Wally Hammond standing behind me and said, 'I know I'm not getting my foot there, but how can I correct the fault?' He immediately replied, 'Never mind your foot; just concentrate on getting your front shoulder round.' I tried his advice with instant, miraculous success!

Another recorded: 'He was a superb judge of what you were doing wrong.' He was also a good judge of which students wanted coaching to raise their game and which were content to be left alone.

The post of sports administrator also involved Hammond in advising on the selection of cricket sides. Moor described Hammond's part in choosing the university team at the beginning of one season:

> At the start of a new academic year, we invited 15 to 20 'freshers' to a special practice. Amongst these were half-a-dozen batsmen who had represented their Provincial Schools teams at Nuffield Week most of whom had struck the ball impressively in the nets. We decided to include three of these batsmen and then showed our proposed team to Wally Hammond. He commented, 'You've left out the best one of the lot.' On pressing him further, he quoted a youngster who had not represented his Provincial School side and had not particularly impressed us. We re-arranged our team and included this youngster as an opening bat for the coming fixture. If I recall correctly, he carried his bat with 70 not out in a score of just under 200, and ended the season top of the averages and our most consistent batsman!

Within weeks of his appointment, Hammond was managing the Natal University side in the Inter-Universities week at Johannesburg. He came to the Wanderers Ground – not the original one where he had played so often but a new centre of South African cricket – 'still a beautifully proportioned 56-year-old, his thick brown hair streaked with grey, and almost unrecognised,' according to the *Daily News*. Charles Fortune, the commentator, knew he was there and, the paper reported, 'held a group of students enthralled with descriptions of Test matches in which Hammond had played while Hammond himself sat a few yards away alone and unencumbered by acolytes.' Marshall Lee, captain of that Natal side, recalled both his modesty and his enthusiasm in declaring, 'he was totally absorbed in the games.' Of Hammond's work as a university manager, the young captain wrote in the Johannesburg *Sunday Times* during the cricket week: 'He has fathered, mothered and guided us. No task, no detail has been too small for him to tackle and he has earned our lasting respect and devotion. He has done more for us than any cricket manager probably has ever done for a team.' Youthful, extravagant language but evoking a hero-worship which the future journalist never lost in the five years he was to know Hammond. Hammond was also involved in selecting the South African Universities Combined side at the end of the annual Universities week in the years in which Natal University was host. Fortune adjudged his qualities as a selector to be 'genius in the council chamber' and Gillie Andrew, another selector, recalled the wisdom of his judgements.

All these activities, of course, involved Hammond in relation-ships with people, something at which he had not always excelled in earlier years. Many students of those Natal days have spoken with respect and affection of their association with him. They were possibly a little overawed! One wrote:

> Though the achievements and reputation of the famous man were so familiar to us that we always thought of him and spoke of him as 'Wally Hammond', it was unthinkable for most of us to address him in any other fashion than as 'Sir' or, perhaps, 'Mr Hammond'.
>
> Even at this stage – I think he was then close to 60 years of age – he had an imposing presence. Large, strongly built and upright, he exuded an air of authority as he strolled around the playing fields, even though I cannot recall ever having seen him walking briskly at this stage. The imagination easily brought to life those many photographs of the powerful athlete 20 to 30 years previously, striding out to face the Australian Test match attack. The steady eyes, strong jawline and broad shoulders were still there.

In his student days Professor Gavin Maasdorp, another Natal University captain of those years and later president of the University Sports Union, saw a great deal of Hammond and commented, 'when you got to know him, he was extremely pleasant but it took a bit of effort.' Hammond had not shed entirely the reserve of a lifetime.

With the academic and administrative staff his relations were less close. One of them felt the real link he had was with students who 'accepted his authority, looked up to him, and appreciated a man of his calibre.' To another academic of those years he was 'a great asset in an expanding job', to a secretary, 'the gentleman with the hearty laugh'. As in earlier years, Hammond presented a smart appearance and a presence. Professor Maasdorp again: 'He would be seen in dark trousers, olive-green shirt, tie or cravat and sports coat – a regal bearing right to the end. Something about him caught your eye.'

The effect of the Natal University job on Hammond himself is important. He was given a new lease of life, brought back in a very real way into a cricket atmosphere, involved with people he found congenial, held in high respect and doing a job to which he was so much more suited than selling motor-cars.

The most remarkable feature of Hammond's work at Natal University was the relationship he struck with the man who had chosen him, Owen Horwood. Horwood, as we have seen, had admired Hammond with all the hero-worship of the devotee. Had he demonstrably shown this, Hammond would have retreated. As Hammond had said many years earlier, he knew that admiration was meant well but it embarrassed him . Horwood was too shrewd for this. He was content to allow the supreme cricketer to grow naturally into the role of sports administrator. The friendship which emerged was possibly the closest Hammond ever made in his life. When Hammond died, Horwood wrote to Maasdorp, 'I don't suppose we can ever hope to replace him here.'

Seventeen years later, Horwood's affection and admiration were undimmed. By 1982 a busy politician and influential cabinet minister, he nevertheless gave me a full evening of his time and summed up his recollections:

Once he had one's confidence, Wally became a true friend. I relied on him completely. He was a man of some force of character, con- sistently charming and modest. The students liked him and had a high regard for him. He was unassuming with them yet gave an impression of authority when needed. I never heard him talk in derogatory terms of anyone. He invariably saw the best in people and he had time to chat to them unhurriedly. He left a fine name in the university. What he did for cricket there and, by example, for South African University cricket and South African cricket as a whole, is immeasurable. From his 'nursery' came six Springbok Test players. My association with

Hammond was one of the most pleasant things of my University career. It was a privilege to know him.

Behind the scenes, making a home in Durban in fair weather and foul, had been Sybil. She had learned over the years to cope with Wally's restlessness. She was used to laying out a garden only to have him want to move. Their third house in Durban, to which they moved just after his university appointment, was in Park Lane, Kloof. The three children went to Kloof High School in the 1960s. As they grew up into young people so they came to know, though not closely, their late-middle-aged father.

One warm summer's evening in Johannesburg in 1982, Valerie recalled for me that childhood as her own little boy, Wally's grandson, played on the lawn. 'I remember helping him with some brick-laying and Roger being taught to fish. There were picnics and trips to the beach.' Looking back at her memories of the man who died when she was 13, she saw him as 'someone with charisma, who attracted people', but she also wished she had known him better. 'He found it difficult to express his feelings to us.' Even to his own children, there was still something of that reserve which others so frequently detected. But Valerie remembered it as a happy home and her mother working hard to make it so. Sybil was closer to the children than was her husband: 'He was a good father, his children never wanted for anything and he loved them all dearly, but he found it difficult to become too involved with their outside activities,' she recalled. It tended to be Sybil rather than Wally who went the round of school functions – prize-giving, sports day, concerts.

Cricket was almost a taboo subject in the household to the extent that Roger as a small boy scarcely knew his father had been a performer. To a master at school who asked him if he was going to be as famous as his father, the boy replied, 'My father played soccer, sir.' True, of course, but scarcely the point! That incident was in 1957, during the period of the 1950s when cricket was almost non-existent for Hammond. When the game came back into his life at the end of the decade, the old enthusiasm returned. At Sybil's instigation, a net was constructed in the new garden at the Park Lane house in Kloof and small boys from the neighbourhood came to be coached. Hammond's approach to his own son was sensible: he gave him a little help but let the boy go his own way in both cricket and rugby. Denis Compton, often in South

Africa in those years, sent his own son, Patrick, along to the coaching classes.

Hammond's accident had led him, during the long weeks of recovery, to take up a hobby which engrossed him for hours. Sybil watched him making model ships. 'It amazed me to see him handling the tiny components; the gentleness with which he would handle the completed article, the look of achievement in his face, a gentleness of touch in a man whose hands and arms were so powerful that a cuddle to the children when young could be in danger of being a massive bear-hug.' The family were briefly separated when Hammond returned to England in May 1962 to help Gloucestershire in a membership drive. The county were immensely grateful for his hard work, which included speaking at functions throughout Gloucestershire.

Hammond continued to have his golfing friends, among them Haydn Bradfield, a future mayor of Durban and brother-in-law of Arthur Coy, South Africa's delegate to the Imperial Cricket Conference. His jovial, extrovert manner made him in many ways the opposite of Hammond, of whom he said, 'he could be charm itself and extremely good company.' Bradfield's persuasiveness led Wally to take part in a game of cricket as late as 1964. He discovered that Hammond had been driving off quietly to watch the farmers play at Richmond, unbeknown to anyone there. He invited him to turn out for a Durban Press Cricket Club XI against an Invitation XI at Richmond. Compton, D. B. Carr and John Woodcock, *The Times* correspondent and later editor of *Wisden*, also played. Compton got 42 and Carr 57. Bradfield recalls the occasion:

> Wally took up his old position in the slips. The crowd who had come to see the legendary figure of England cricket were almost rewarded when he just missed a sharp snick for which he apologised profusely. When he went in to bat, everyone hoped for just one cover drive. After he had made a few, he lofted a catch which he believed (wrongly!) was dropped on purpose. He therefore gave his wicket away a few overs later. When the game was over, he stayed for the braai (barbeque), and declared he had enjoyed his day.

He drove back to Durban in the starlight of a warm December evening, the majestic cricketer who had played his last game.

That match at Richmond had coincided with the visit of the MCC party, many of whom had gone to watch the game. Ted Dexter met him then and commented, 'He could not have been nicer or more straightforward. He did have that certain air about him and you could imagine him doing all those imperious things which people attribute to him.' Gradually he had been drawn into the company of the younger men. He was invited into the dressing room for the Test at Durban and a few days later he was again involved when he chose the South African Universities side which played MCC at Pietermaritzburg. He enjoyed the game but regretted that the South African Universities captain ignored his advice to field first. In choosing to bat, the undergraduates were straightaway up against the class bowling of J. S. E. Price, D. J. Brown and D. A. Allen. They lost 5 wickets for 51, never really recovered and lost by an innings. When MCC came to Port Elizabeth for the last Test, in February 1965, they asked Walter and Sybil to be their guests. Hammond's last sight of English cricket was a century by the rising star, Geoffrey Boycott. In the closing weeks of his life, he had become again a part of the scene he had so often adorned.

His old cricketing and golfing friend and colleague, 'Gubby' Allen, was out for the tour. Allen recalled a last dinner they had together, an occasion both nostalgic and sad. The two men, close in age with a cricketing experience shared over forty years – they had first played against each other in 1923 – reminisced. 'He was charming, that evening,' his host remarked, 'but the mental and physical scars of his accident were there. The finely built man I had known was no more.' But he was softer, the profiles of his outlook on life less severely drawn, the memories of past players kinder. Allen had been grateful for the meeting. 'I was fond of Wally and perhaps I was lucky enough always to see the better side of him.'

A few weeks later, the 1964–65 season ended with a dinner at the university, at which tributes were paid both to Horwood, now the university's vice-chancellor, and to Hammond. It was the first such function. The chairman remarked: 'When the guest speaker rises at the fiftieth one, it will be sufficient for him to say that Walter Hammond was there at the start.' As the mild winter approached, Hammond was less on the cricket field and more in his office. The new vice-chancellor would ask his sports administrator to share a sandwich lunch with him from time to time to discuss the next stages of development in university sport. He had set out in 1959, Horwood said, 'not merely to keep students fit, but to instil into them adherence to the principles of sportsmanship and the development of a healthy outlook.' Much had been achieved by 1965 and, as Dr Horwood told me in 1982, 'Wally and I had had still greater plans for the future.' Under their particular aegis, this was not to be. On 1 July 1965, after a heart attack and a few hours' illness, Walter Hammond died at the age of 62.

He had given much to cricket in those last six years. In the opinion of Boon Wallace, a past vice-president of the South African Cricket Union, he had pioneered the role of sports administrators in South African universities. At Natal, Hammond was succeeded by Trevor Goddard, a former Springbok captain. Other universities made similar appointments and the standards which were produced had a major effect on the contribution of university cricket to the game at provincial and international level.

Strangely, no overtures were made to involve Hammond directly in South African cricket at first-class level. 'We would have welcomed him in any capacity,' said Alan Melville. Yet the regret remains that no invitation was made, and Hammond was not the man to offer his own services. A persuasive voice from the Natal administrators in, say, 1952 or, better, 1959, might have won a response. As it was, South African cricket benefited at one remove rather than directly from the last six years of his life.

Let the last word on the South African years come from one of his students writing in the Johannesburg *Sunday Chronicle* a few days after his death: 'No matter how intense the feeling, I can hardly do more than scant justice to the greatness of the man.'

11
Majesty

'He enriched the game with a grace, a
simplicity and a nobility that may
never be seen again.'

Wisden, 1942.

The cricket world stopped in its tracks on the first weekend of July
1965 to pay its tribute to Walter Hammond. In the *Guardian*,
Neville Cardus, who had recognised his abilities over 40 years
earlier, put him in his World XI of all time. E. W. Swanton, in the
Daily Telegraph, called him 'the most majestic presence that ever
graced a cricket field since WG.' The *Bristol Citizen* carried a
front-page banner headline, 'Hammond, the cricket genius, dies.
Greatest all-rounder of all time.' His place in history was assured.

Later that month a memorial service was held in Bristol
Cathedral. 'It is hard indeed to evaluate the sum of human
happiness created by Walter Hammond's cricket,' declared
Viscount Cobham, the former Worcestershire captain. The fully
choral service was conducted by the Bishop of Malmesbury and
the lesson was read by the Duke of Beaufort. The president and
secretary of MCC were present and cricketers past and present,
home and overseas, were represented. The only family mourner
able to come was Mrs Marion Hammond, who was to outlive her
son by five years.

On over 1000 occasions in first-class cricket and on countless
others in minor or wartime games, Hammond had left some
pavilion to go out and bat. The chances were that he might
have been reading a book, as absorbed in its pages as he would
presently be in batting. Majesty, they said, strode to the wicket.

'I've seen a world-beater,' Joe Hardstaff senior told his son, the first time he umpired in Hammond's company. Power, grace, timing, style and speed were translated into his cover drive, caught for ever by that famous picture. Whether he played off the front foot or the back foot made no difference. In an arc between cover and mid-wicket no fielder was safe from his onslaught. Bill Voce singled out the 336 against New Zealand for the sheer fear it aroused in the hearts of anyone near at hand. 'On his day,' said that bowler feelingly, 'it didn't matter where you bowled to him.' His armour might perhaps be pierced by a short, fast ball lifting into his body but only from bowlers of the highest quality. His overall authority over them was defied only by O'Reilly and his command of strokes only qualified by a responsible reluctance to hook. G. O. Allen thought him the greatest off-side player he ever saw and the finest player of spin-bowling.

Hammond also bowled. The ball swung late, sometimes with a lot of pace, faster off the pitch than expected. The run-up was modest, economical, without threat, and the body movement relaxed, sideways in action, composed. Hutton called him the most graceful swing-bowler he ever saw, Bradman believed that he could have been as great as Maurice Tate or Alec Bedser. Great players in the game were his victims. He bowled for England rather than for Gloucestershire, and in the earlier rather than the later years. But he bowled enough to be acclaimed by the press so often in the 1920s and 1930s 'the great all-rounder', despite the fact that he never did the double.

It was Charlie Parker of Gloucestershire who put the Cirencester schoolboy in the slips to end an epidemic of dropped catches. There he stayed throughout his career, erect, still, evenly balanced, well-placed, watchful, tigerish. He anticipated the stroke yet to be made. The ball was caught before the onlooker realised. Daring to pass him, it was retrieved like some errant child brought back to account. Without fuss or gimmickry, with flannels unstained, the deed was done.

From the moment he went onto the field he was in command. 'One hardly had eyes for any other player' was a typical comment. Fellow-players were conscious of this. Tom Graveney confessed that on the one occasion they played together, he himself 'could hardly bat for the presence of the man. His sheer charisma affected everyone on the field.' Sir Donald Bradman remembered 'a superb athletic figure, beautifully attired'. The creamy shirts, immaculate flannels, blue handkerchief casually exposed, would be exchanged off the field for well-cut Savile Row suits. This very masculine man had almost a feminine pedantry about his appearance. Only in his love of a favourite trilby, worn long after its prime was over and finally disposed of by Sybil, did he fall below his own standards of sartorial excellence.

There has survived the record, like some piece of discovered film, of a conversation-piece in the Long Room at Lord's in 1934 in which a group unanimously placed Hammond as 'the greatest of them all'. Neville Cardus, a couple of years later, turned the statement into a question, leaving posterity to find an answer. As early as 1927 Cardus had written, 'there is no going beyond perfection and Hammond's back strokes are not less than perfect.' He listed the men of 1905 and declared that Hammond would have been a 'bright light in their company'. From Cardus it was an immaculate bestowal of praise. He was a writer for whom the Whig theory of historical progress worked in reverse: cricketers, in general, got worse.

C. B. Fry, half a generation older than Cardus, had played with those Golden Age cricketers. Indeed, his own casting vote in 1899 had ended Grace's career in Test matches. He was still watching the game after Hutton had retired and he believed Hammond to be 'the greatest batsman of them all'. John Arlott has argued that the claims of Sir Jack Hobbs were even stronger: 'Those who played with him and against him generally considered him – in all conditions, on all pitches, and against all types of bowling – the finest batsman.' A later generation will accredit Sir Garfield Sobers, Ian Botham and Vivian Richards. They in their day have been crowd-winners as Hammond had been before them. His greatness, as Cardus never tired of saying, lay in his art.

Hammond's grace and movement were more enduring things than the fortunes of the games he played in. In an age which had not yet come to demand instant pleasure, rapid results and constant excitement, he was utterly acceptable. His artistry, cast in the 1980s, would have adorned cricket's most spectacular occasions. During a one-day final at Lord's in 1982, I asked Sir Leonard Hutton where Hammond stood in the gallery of the great. He had paused in answering some of my earlier questions. This time there was no pause. The answer came back unequivocally: 'I find it hard to rate anyone higher.'

Hammond had the edge on Bradman and Hobbs because of the

extra dimension of bowling. As fielders, all three were exemplary. But measurement in the pursuit of cricketing comparisons is fruitless. We may prove that A could jump higher than B and that X could swim faster than Y. But even if we agree that Larwood bowled faster than Spofforth and was himself eclipsed by Lillee, what have we established? Aggregates of runs and wickets enable the leaders to distance themselves from the rest of the pack but they do not establish absolute judgements. The statistics remain to be enjoyed, even to tantalise. They are not our masters.

Hammond became the first professional to turn amateur and captain England. In the 1920s he had found it hard to accept the social gulf which existed between professionals and amateurs. He was unusual in calling his county captain of the 1930s by his Christian name rather than 'sir'. Curiously, there were young professionals who felt more at ease calling him 'Mr Hammond' even in his professional days. The second world war, which changed economic patterns and social attitudes, led to the end of the absurdity of those divisions. Hammond did more than anyone else to help to bring this about and to make it possible eventually for a professional (while still a professional) to captain England. Today the concept of amateurs, with their initials before their names, belongs to the archives.

Yet the unanimity of opinion on his skills as a player are not matched by the verdict on his captaincy. A line must be drawn between him as a captain before and after the war. In the two home series and the overseas tour of South Africa before 1939 his leadership won more praise than blame from opponents, journalists and colleagues. Alan Melville had admired his control of a fielding side, the young Jeffrey Stollmeyer had noticed his skill as a tactician, Leslie Ames had felt he had no rival. The South African writer Louis Duffus called his captaincy 'exemplary'. Sir Pelham Warner, admittedly a biassed commentator since Hammond could do nothing wrong in his eyes, felt the same: 'That he was immensely liked and appreciated by his side is certain and he was understanding and sympathetic to those who failed.' Hammond himself had admired the qualities of three pre-war Test captains under whom he served – the brilliance and flamboyance of Chapman, the courage and dedication of Jardine and the personality and efficiency of G. O. Allen. While Chapman's style could scarcely be his own, he drew strongly on the qualities of Jardine and Allen. His brief experience as Gloucestershire's captain in

1939 raised the county many places in the Championship. Here he learnt from B. O. Allen and from Lyon. 'I had no complaints,' said his county colleague, Sinfield.

After the war his captaincy is principally associated with the tour of Australia. His opposite number was Bradman who, in the view of several of Hammond's colleagues, out-manoeuvred him as a tactician. The two men had a different approach. For Bradman, it was another encounter for the Ashes with no holds barred. For Hammond it was a goodwill tour. Their philosophies were the wrong way round. Bradman could conceivably have shown the goodwill as leader of the stronger side. Hammond, leading the weaker team, was in no position to give quarter.

Off the field, the commendable qualities he had shown before the war were lacking. Sir Donald Bradman told me, 'I felt he showed little imagination and did not display the leadership and tact required of an overseas diplomat which international captains on overseas trips are required to do.' The man who had welcomed the England captaincy in 1937 found it less appealing in 1947. Denis Compton believed that 'the players looked to the captain for guidance and it was not there.' These may be seen as the hardest judgements against him.

The biographer must offer some explanation for this complete change in attitude. As soon as Hammond had to worry about his performance as a player, captaincy became a burden. He felt strangely out of tune and unable to communicate with the younger men whom he led in 1946–47. He wrote, 'they are sitting impatiently waiting for their turn, so many of whom I have enjoyed helping along.' Yet what he could say in print he found difficult to put into practice. Compton again: 'His silence was a new experience to me.' Washbrook believed that the answer lay in the team he led. 'He could have been a great captain of a great side,' he remarked. Getting the best out of an indifferent side required him to make allowances for the qualities of others. Even when his own performances had fallen from the peak, he still found it difficult to know how to encourage others. His captaincy was affected by his own abilities.

In summary, when he was riding high, captaincy presented no problems. In the brief post-war period, poor health, disappointing performance and domestic worries took their toll. Though we are reminded that Bradman had to contend with poorer health, yet he was the tougher man. For all Hammond's physical strength, he had not the imperturbability of spirit which is part of the quality of toughness.

Marie Lloyd had spotted so long ago the character of the shy boy who had wanted to do nothing more in life than hit a cricket ball. He had never lost his shyness, as Grace James had observed. He had danced well but said little. The story is told of a young officer who danced with Agatha Christie, the novelist, when she was very young. At the end he took her back to her mother with the reproach, 'Your daughter dances well. Now you must teach her to talk.' Had someone given that advice to Wally Hammond (perhaps they did) he might have been less misunderstood and just as great. Women spotted the problem rather than men. They saw, as Muriel Pannell and her mother had done, the transition from 'a youth with a shy but lovable nature' to a talented middle-aged man who screened himself from all but a few. His second wife felt she had to protect him from an anonymous but admiring world and guide him towards where real friends might be found.

Those who cast him as their schoolboy hero, as many young cricketers did, got scant return for their pains. He never talked to Washbrook in his first Test. Stollmeyer accepted his aloofness as the privilege of the older man: 'I would not have expected otherwise. Be that as it may, all men are different and great men deservedly so.'

His critics have commented on his reluctance to coach. It was something I discussed with Sir Leonard Hutton, who approached the subject by suggesting what it was like to bat with him. 'It was sheer delight, and I batted with him many times. You felt you were receiving instruction in the best possible way. It was like a man planing a piece of wood – the master-craftsman doing it for you to watch. There was no patter needed.' For those lucky enough to be at the other end of the wicket or on the fielding side, here was a *de luxe* coaching lesson. But what of the player less fortunately placed? Hutton went on, 'He would have hesitated to offer advice. There never was a more modest fellow. I knew that if I wanted an opinion, I only had to ask. Not everyone can teach by talking. Hammond taught by simply showing.' The young men at Natal University, at the end of his days, had to wrest advice out of him when part of his appointment was specifically to coach. We are brought back to his shyness, not confronted with indifference. What he preached on coaching in his books he found hard to practise. But the intent was there and the same spirit was true of his attitude to supporters. He could write of the warmth and friend-liness of thousands of unknown friends to whom he was anxious to give of the best. Example triumphed over gesture. He played many a game, beyond the call of professional duty, in evening charity appearances. There was a long trip to Cornwall when, almost crippled with pain, he batted with a runner. It was an offering made without complaint.

For some of those who came to watch him, the pleasing gesture was the autograph. Hammond's approach to these requests related to his mood. On the whole, he was much more likely to sign autographs on the unofficial occasions than during a first-class match but he might be caught near the tea-tent at some county game and let a group of youngsters swarm over him. In the great years of the 1930s, a Yorkshire lad got his autograph at Headingley during a Test with the smiling comment, 'Pity your Herbert isn't playing, son.' When his career was over, he was stopped in the milling crowds during a Lord's Test lunch interval in 1948 by a man paying his first visit there and he willingly signed in the back page of a diary.

The cricketers of Hammond's day never became rich. As a young man he had struggled to find £12 to meet an income tax demand and had done so by winning at the Cheltenham races. For most of his professional days he was worth about £10 a week. The early years of his first marriage, his benefit year and his business career all brought increased income but his total earnings in a lifetime were under £75,000. He saved little. Clothes and cars mattered, his mother got some help, he paid his round of drinks, he moved in circles more affluent than his own. When he died there was no provision for Sybil and the children.

Gloucestershire at once launched an Appeal which had the support of the Dukes of Norfolk and Beaufort and a large number of distinguished administrators and players. 1500 people responded, contributing some £3500, one of the largest donations coming from a collection at his old school at Cirencester. A Trust Fund was set up, intended to benefit both the Hammond family and the dependants of other first-class cricketers. Sybil Hammond, whose children at the time of her husband's death were all teen-agers, continued to make her home in South Africa apart from a brief visit to England in the late 1960s when she lived in Dursley in Gloucestershire.

Wally Hammond may not have made a lot of money nor found

it easy to make a lot of friends. He had his fair share of human weaknesses. He drove too fast, but his near-fatal accident was not his fault; he smoked too much, but anti-smoking policies were in their infancy; he enjoyed alcohol, but knew when to stop; he had an eye for pretty women, but was not promiscuous. On the other hand he possessed in abundance qualities of sportsmanship, integrity and honesty and he gave to the game of cricket dignity and style.

During the second world war, A. E. R. Gilligan wrote, 'W. G. Grace drew all England to him and made cricket a national game. Jack Hobbs saved it after the first world war. Walter Hammond has kept the torch brightly burning in these dark and difficult days.' We may add some words of Robertson-Glasgow, also written during the war but referring to the peacetime years, to give us all the epitaph we need: 'He enriched the game with a grace, a simplicity and a nobility that may never be seen again.'

Yet in the end we are left with the image of a man who gave happiness to thousands but who never quite secured a fair share for himself; whose mastery of technique delighted the purists but whose philosophy of life faltered; who amassed runs yet failed to amass the personal assurance which men crave; whose cover drive was a gift from the gods but whose craftsmanship in the building of relationships showed human frailty. He was a great public figure but a very private person.

Statistical Appendix

For Gloucestershire

BATTING

Opponents	Inns	N.O.	Runs	H.S.	Ave.	50s	100s	Catches
Derbyshire	37	3	2158	237	63.47	11	6	40
Essex	44	6	1888	244	49.68	4	6	48
Glamorgan	42	7	2774	302*	79.25	6	10	28
Hampshire	44	2	1576	192	37.52	11	3	31
Kent	48	3	2352	290	52.26	14	6	35
Lancashire	47	4	2823	271	65.65	6	10	33
Leicestershire	27	2	1460	252	58.40	4	5	24
Middlesex	49	5	2398	178	54.50	9	8	47
Northamptonshire	13	3	796	193	79.60	3	3	15
Nottinghamshire	28	3	1935	317	77.40	1	10	38
Somerset	43	9	2483	214	73.02	11	10	41
Surrey	37	3	2066	205*	60.76	3	11	35
Sussex	42	2	1627	168*	40.67	10	4	24
Warwickshire	32	4	1545	238*	55.17	8	3	22
Worcestershire	44	5	1946	265*	49.89	7	6	45
Yorkshire	42	5	1517	162*	41.00	4	5	24
Cambridge University	3	1	228	113*	114.00	–	2	1
Oxford University	16	2	915	211*	65.35	6	2	9
Australians	6	–	169	89	28.16	2	–	1
Indians	6	2	194	81	48.50	1	–	2
New Zealanders	3	–	183	108	61.00	–	1	–
South Africans	4	1	232	123	77.33	1	1	2
West Indians	7	2	399	264	79.80	–	1	6
	664	74	33,664	317	57.05	122	113	551

BOWLING

Opponents	Balls	Mdns	Runs	Wkts	Ave.	5 wkts/ inns	10 wkts/ match
Derbyshire	1742	72	675	17	39.70	1	–
Essex	2595	97	1180	38	31.05	–	–
Glamorgan	2645	108	1149	47	24.44	1	1
Hampshire	2886	118	1271	60	21.18	3	–
Kent	2139	67	1049	29	36.17	–	–
Lancashire	2262	101	897	25	35.88	–	–

Opponents	Balls	Mdns	Runs	Wkts	Ave.	5 wkts/ inns	10 wkts/ match
Leicestershire	1614	70	658	25	26.32	1	–
Middlesex	2906	102	1363	45	30.28	1	–
Northamptonshire	1028	46	415	15	27.66	–	–
Nottinghamshire	889	37	378	11	34.36	–	–
Somerset	1764	80	666	25	26.24	1	–
Surrey	1748	65	787	29	27.13	2	–
Sussex	2364	98	1031	39	26.43	3	1
Warwickshire	1327	45	669	9	74.33	–	–
Worcestershire	1980	83	807	38	21.23	2	1
Yorkshire	1741	76	813	23	35.34	–	–
Cambridge University	105	5	55	4	13.75	–	–
Oxford University	732	30	364	11	33.09	–	–
Australians	114	3	100	–	–	–	–
Indians	421	19	169	4	42.25	–	–
New Zealanders	30	2	4	–	–	–	–
South Africans	366	7	186	7	26.57	–	–
West Indians	204	2	115	3	38.33	–	–
	33,602	1333	14,801	504	29.36	15	3

For England

BATTING

Opponents	Matches	Inns	N.O.	Runs	H.S.	Ave.	50s	100s	Catches
Australia	33	58	3	2852	251	51.85	7	9	43
West Indies	13	20	2	639	138	35.50	1	1	22
South Africa	24	42	7	2188	181	62.51	14	6	30
New Zealand	9	11	2	1015	336*	112.77	1	4	9
India	6	9	2	555	217	79.28	1	2	6
	85	140	16	7249	336*	58.45	24	22	110

BOWLING

Opponents	Balls	Mdns	Runs	Wkts	Ave.	5 wkts/ inns	10 wkts/ match
Australia	3958	135	1612	36	44.77	1	–
West Indies	414	15	176	3	59.33	–	–
South Africa	2811	122	1041	34	30.61	–	–
New Zealand	505	19	188	6	31.33	–	–
India	279	8	121	4	30.25	–	–
	7967	299	3138	83	37.83	1	–

All first-class cricket

BATTING

Season	Matches	Inns	N.O.	Runs	H.S.	Ave.	50s	100s	Catches
In England									
1920	3	4	1	27	18	9.00	–	–	–
1921	2	3	–	2	1	0.66	–	–	–
1922	5	9	–	88	32	9.77	–	–	8
1923	29	55	4	1421	110	27.86	8	1	21
1924	27	45	4	1239	174*	30.21	4	2	30
1925	33	58	5	1818	250*	34.30	9	3	65
1926				(did not play owing to illness)					
1927	34	47	4	2969	197	69.04	12	12	46
1928	35	48	5	2825	244	65.69	15	9	78
1929	28	47	9	2456	238*	64.63	8	10	36
1930	27	44	6	2032	211*	53.47	8	5	31
1931	32	49	7	1781	168*	42.40	5	6	46
1932	30	49	4	2528	264	56.17	9	8	50
1933	34	54	5	3323	264	67.81	8	13	54
1934	23	35	4	2366	302*	76.32	5	8	23
1935	35	58	5	2616	252	49.35	12	7	54
1936	25	42	5	2107	317	56.94	10	5	13
1937	33	55	5	3252	217	65.04	15	13	38
1938	26	42	2	3011	271	75.27	7	15	33
1939	28	46	7	2479	302	63.56	7	7	35
1945	6	10	–	592	121	59.20	2	3	11
1946	19	26	5	1783	214	84.90	9	7	19
1950	1	2	1	107	92*	107.00	1	–	1
1951	1	1	–	7	7	7.00	–	–	–
In Australia and New Zealand									
1928–29	13	18	1	1553	251	91.35	1	7	10
1932–33	15	21	2	1569	336*	82.58	6	5	16
1936–37	14	23	2	1242	231*	59.14	4	5	11
1946–47	13	19	–	781	208	41.10	2	2	12
In South Africa									
1927–28	14	21	2	908	166*	47.78	4	2	13
1930–31	13	19	2	1045	136*	61.47	7	3	18
1938–39	15	18	1	1025	181	60.29	4	4	15
1942–43	1	2	–	78	60	39.00	1	–	2
In West Indies									
1925–26	10	18	3	732	238*	48.80	2	2	15
1934–35	10	17	3	789	281*	56.35	–	3	15
All First-Class Matches	634	1005	104	50,551	336*	56.10	185	167	819

BOWLING

Season	Balls	Mdns	Runs	Wkts	Ave.	5 wkts/ inns	10 wkts/ match
In England							
1921	60	–	76	–	–	–	–
1922	6	–	8	–	–	–	–
1923	1392	41	742	18	41.22	1	–
1924	1845	69	775	29	26.72	–	–
1925	4081	146	2003	68	29.45	1	–
1926	(did not play owing to illness)						
1927	1644	55	884	20	44.20	–	–
1928	4323	168	1941	84	23.10	6	2
1929	2070	84	978	28	34.92	–	–
1930	2436	105	928	30	30.93	1	–
1931	3549	138	1457	47	31.00	1	–
1932	3767	176	1483	53	27.98	–	–
1933	3196	115	1375	38	36.18	2	1
1934	2371	94	1059	21	50.42	–	–
1935	3702	142	1636	60	27.26	–	–
1936	2540	108	1047	41	25.53	1	–
1937	2521	68	1094	48	22.79	2	–
1938	2060	82	847	14	60.50	–	–
1939	72	1	39	3	13.00	–	–
1945	–	–	–	–	–	–	–
1946	36	3	14	1	14.00	–	–
1950	66	3	25	–	–	–	–
In Australia and New Zealand							
1928–29	1600	50	661	11	60.09	–	–
1932–33	1429	38	597	20	29.85	1	–
1936–37	1571	27	577	27	21.37	2	–
1946–47	24	–	8	–	–	–	–
In South Africa							
1927–28	1500	58	644	27	23.85	2	–
1930–31	1330	51	494	15	32.93	–	–
1938–39	776	23	260	7	37.14	–	–
1942–43	16	1	5	–	–	–	–
In West Indies							
1925–26	1188	42	573	20	28.65	2	–
1934–35	342	11	161	2	80.50	–	–
All First-Class Matches	51,513	1,899	22,391	732	30.58	22	3

A Note on Sources

Newspapers

The first-class career of W. R. Hammond was reported in every newspaper which regarded cricket as part of its sporting province. Whether or not a particular game might be given a syndicated summary or a specialised commentary depended on many factors, not least the decision of an editor to send one of his staff to watch. The files of newspaper offices themselves and the resources of the Bodleian Library, Oxford, the Bristol City Library, and the British Museum Newspaper Section at Colindale made it possible for me to consult the following. Some also throw light on Hammond's career as a schoolboy, in charity games and during the second world war.

The *Age* (Melbourne)
The *All Sports Weekly*
The *Barbados Advocate*
The *Bristol Evening Post*
The *Bristol Observer*
The *Bristol Times and Mirror*
The *Cape Times*
The *Cheltenham Chronicle*
The *Cheltenham and Gloucester Echo*
The *Cirencestrian*
The *Daily Argosy* (British Guiana)
The *Daily Express*
The *Daily Gleaner* (Jamaica)
The *Daily Herald*
The *Daily Mail*
The *Daily Sketch*
The *Daily Telegraph* (and *Morning Post*)
The *Evening News*
The *Evening Standard*
The *Star*
The *Gloucester Citizen*
The *Graphic*
The *Illustrated London News*
The *Illustrated Sporting News*

The *(Manchester) Guardian*
The *Melbourne Herald*
The *Natal Daily News*
The *Natal Mercury*
The *News Chronicle*
The *News of the World*
The *People*
The *Picture Post*
The *Rand Daily Mail*
The *Sporting Globe* (Melbourne)
The *Sun* (Sydney)
The *Sunday Chronicle* (Johannesburg)
The *Sunday Dispatch*
The *Sunday Express*
The *Sunday Times*
The *Sunday Times* (Johannesburg)
The *Sydney Morning Herald*
The *Sydney Sun*
The Times
The *Weekly Dispatch*
The *Western Daily Press*
The *Western Morning Post*
The *Wiltshire and Gloucestershire Standard*

Books and Journals

Apart from newspapers, the main sources for Hammond's career are *Wisden's Cricketers' Almanack* (see especially 1942 and 1966) and *The Cricketer*.

Few cricket books relating to the inter-war years can avoid a reference to Hammond. The following were consulted in the writing of this biography:

Altham, H. S. & Swanton, E. W., *A History of Cricket*, 1926 *et al*.
Ames, L. E. G., *Close of Play*, 1953
Bedser, A. V., *Cricket Choice*, 1981
Bradman, Sir Donald, *Farewell to Cricket*, 1950
Caple, S. G., *History of Gloucestershire County Cricket*, 1949
Cardus, Sir Neville, *Close of Play*, 1956
Cardus, Sir Neville, *Days in the Sun*, 1924
Cardus, Sir Neville, *Good Days*, 1934
Cardus, Sir Neville, *The Playfair Cardus*, 1963

Cary, Clif, *Cricket Controversy*, 1947

Coldham, J. D., *Lord Harris*, 1983

Compton, D. C. S. & Edrich, W. J., *Cricket and All That*, 1978

Compton, D. C. S., *Compton on Cricketers*, 1980

Compton, D. C. S., *'Testing Time' for England*, 1948

Dexter, E. R., *From Bradman to Boycott*, 1980

Edrich, W. J., *Cricket Heritage*, 1948

Edrich, W. J., *Cricketing Days*, 1950

Farnes, Kenneth, *Tours and Tests*, 1940

Fender, P. G. H., *Turn of the Wheel*, 1929

Fingleton, J. H., *Batting from Memory*, 1981

Fingleton, J. H., *Cricket Crisis*, 1947

Fry, C. B., *Life Worth Living*, 1939

Hammond, W. R., *Cricket My Destiny*, 1946

Hammond, W. R., *Cricket My World*, 1948

Hammond, W. R., *Cricket's Secret History*, 1952

Hammond, W. R., *Cricketers' School*, 1950

Harris, Bruce, *1937 Australian Test Tour*, 1937

Harris, Bruce, *With England in Australia*, 1947

Hobbs, Sir John, *The Fight for the Ashes, 1932–33*, 1933

Howat, Gerald, *Learie Constantine*, 1975

Hutton, Sir Leonard, *Cricket Is My Life*, 1949

Hutton, Sir Leonard, *Just My Story*, 1956

Jardine, D. R., *In Quest of the Ashes*, 1933

Lee, H. W., *Forty Years of English Cricket*, 1948

Le Quesne, L., *The Bodyline Controversy*, 1983

Mason, Ronald, *Walter Hammond*, 1962

Moore, David, *W. R. Hammond*, 1948

Moyes, A. G., *A Century of Cricket*, 1950

Noble, M. A., *Fight for the Ashes*, 1929

Parker, Grahame, *Gloucestershire Road*, 1983

Sewell, E. H. D., *Cricket up to Date*, 1931

Swanton, E. W., *Follow On*, 1977

Swanton, E. W., *Sort of a Cricket Person*, 1972

Swanton, E. W., *Swanton in Australia*, 1975

Travers, Ben, *Ninety-Four Declared*, 1981

Warner, Sir Pelham, *Cricket Between Two Wars*, 1942

Warner, Sir Pelham, *Lord's*, 1946

Wellings, E. M., *Vintage Cricketers*, 1983

Wyatt, R. E. S., *Ins and Outs*, 1936

Wyatt, R. E. S., *Three Straight Sticks*, 1951

Yardley, N. W. D., *Cricket Campaigns*, 1950

Index